SHAPESHIFTING

SHAPESHIFTING

Shamanic Techniques
for Global and Personal Transformation

JOHN PERKINS

Destiny Books
Rochester, Vermont

Destiny Books
One Park Street
Rochester, Vermont 05767
www.InnerTraditions.com

Destiny Books is a division of Inner Traditions International

LIBRARY OF CONGRESS CATALOGING-IN-PUBLICATION DATA

Perkins, John M.
  Shapeshifting : shamanic techniques for global and personal transformation / John Perkins.
    p.   cm.
  Includes bibliographical references.
  ISBN 0-89281-663-5 (alk. paper)
  1. Shamanism—Miscellanea. 2. Metamorphosis—Miscellanea. 3. Indians of South America—Amazon River Region—Miscellanea. I. Title.
  BF1623.M47P47   1997   97-27280
  291.1'44—dc21   CIP

Printed and bound in Canada

10   9   8   7

This book was typeset in Minion with Matrix Narrow and Neuland Solid as the display typefaces

Contents

Part 2

THE VIEW FROM WITHIN

An immense feeling of strength infused me. It was no longer the illusion of power, which causes one to become weary of the battle and to want to give in. Astrain whispered to me again ... He said that I should always confront the world with the same weapons that were used to challenge me. And that I could confront a dog only by transforming myself into a dog.

Paulo Coelho
The Pilgrimage

To Mom, who taught us during her final forty-five days
that ecstasy is about feeling our oneness,
and who—despite her pain—guided me through
the pages of this book.

Introduction

I was asked to speak at the 1995 International Women's Conference in Miami shortly after my third book was published. Five authors were invited, four of us men. My topic was the potential impact of indigenous women shamans on the future of the world. Four men out of five presenters at the International Women's Conference—something seemed out of balance. I decided to turn my time at the lectern over to a woman.

Although only twelve years old, my daughter Jessica was highly qualified. She first visited indigenous people when she was eight months old; my wife, Winifred, still talks about the time she and and I waited while a group of Mayan women, standing knee deep in a lake where they wash clothes, embroidered skirts tucked into their sashes, passed Jessica around, amazed that such a large baby was less than a year old. Later, Jessica trained with Quechua shamans in the Andes, was initiated during a fire ceremony in the Guatemalan highlands, and was a member of the first group of outsiders ever to visit a remote clan of headhunters deep in the Amazon.

"There are three points I want to make tonight," Jessica told her Miami audience. "First, I feel that my generation was saddled with a burden heavier than that of any other people in history, a legacy of polluting our world to the brink of destruction. Second, changing it will require far more than recycling and other environmental Band-Aids. And third, we women must play a major role. We are the nurturers. Above all else, this transition will be about shifting ourselves into earth-honoring and sustainable ways of living."

I, like the rest of the audience, was deeply moved. More than the others, however, I knew that the credit for Jessica's expansive point of view, and her impassioned plea, belonged to the shapeshifters who had influenced her young life.

Throughout history we humans have found shapeshifting to be one of the most effective means for transforming ourselves, both as individuals and communities. A Lakota Sioux warrior shapeshifted into a buffalo in order to become a better hunter and to honor the spirit of an animal that provided his family with food, clothing, bowstrings, and fuel. Entire tribes adjusted to glaciers, floods, and other environmental changes by radically altering their perceptions and lifestyles.

Modern cultures have exchanged such practices for a belief in man's ability to control the world around him. The hunt has been replaced by industrialized farms, slaughterhouses, and meat-packing factories. Rather than attempting to adjust to flooding rivers, we build levees. Both individuals and communities appear to live apart from what we too often refer to as the "rest of the world" or "nature," as if we were separate from them.

Yet now, poised at the edge of a new millennium, we face a multitude of crises. Painfully aware of our polluted air and water, our inadequacy to combat poverty, and our increasing tendency to resort to violence, suicide, drugs, and other destructive behavior, we wonder what is to come. . . .

But stop! This is not a time to lament the past or despair over the future. It is a time to open the door to all the wonderful possibilities inherent in the awarenesses and technologies developed over the past decades. This is a time for optimism.

We are the first people in history to harness the miracles of physics, inhabit homes with heating and air conditioning, travel to the moon, and watch it all on television. We know what we have—and what we miss. We are the first to be able to make rational choices about the trade-offs involved in development—to say that, based on actual experience, the fruits of economic expansion are not always worth the price. Never before have any citizens of this planet been in a position to evaluate the benefits (and costs) of power plants that generate electricity (and greenhouse gases), highways that unite us (and destroy our once-sacred land), or chemicals that provide amazing diversity on supermarket shelves and department store racks (and poison our rivers and bodies).

Ours is a time of great hope because we have learned so much about ourselves and our relation to our home. Our "giant leap for mankind" may be symbolized by Neil Armstrong's footprint on the moon, but it took thousands of years for us to get there, and, in the process, we proved that we are not the masters of the universe. Although that footprint is an indelible symbol, the real leap was deep inside our psyches. When we took it, we entered a realm that offers an extraordinary opportunity for us to change ourselves.

This book is about change—shapeshifting—in all its forms.

In part 1 you will learn about the different types of shapeshifting, techniques for accomplishing each, and theories regarding how those changes happen. You will discover that we all have the ability to shapeshift on a cellular level, to transform ourselves into jaguars or bushes or any other form with which we create an alliance. Also, each of us can shift into being more of the self we most respect and want to emphasize, bringing about fundamental changes in our attitudes, perceptions, prosperity, health, appearance, and personal relationships.

Part 2 describes remarkable incidents that happened to groups of people traveling with me through the Amazon rainforest, experiences that included each of the different types of shapeshifting discussed in part 1. You will meet respected medical doctors and scientists from the United States who underwent radical changes of body and mind. And you will learn about a profound institutional shapeshift that created a new organization, the type of transformation Jessica called for in her Miami speech.

Throughout parts 1 and 2 you will be introduced to techniques that will enable you to be the shapeshifter; simply follow the directions and examples provided by Viejo Itza and the other shapeshifters.

What follows is a series of stories—all of them true. For me, storytelling is the easiest way to write. And storytelling is part of the shapeshifter's tradition.

Part 1

THE
VIEW
FROM
ABOVE

Chapter 1

The Mayan View

The great stone pyramid rose out of the jungle like a volcano into the morning sky. A monument to endurance, it had defied gods who sent hurricanes across the Gulf of Mexico to destroy it and grave robbers who had hacked away at it for countless centuries, picking it clean of all its jade and gold, leaving only the rocks, the plants that took root along its precipitous walls, and the carved figure at its summit.

It seemed part of the landscape, a cousin of the forest; but the pyramid had been conceived by people, every stone set in place by human hands. It was the creation of a civilization of magicians who had transformed the Yucatan from a tangled jungle into a land of agricultural bounty, splendid cities, and architectural masterpieces.

The Maya drained the swamps. They constructed massive islandlike platforms in the marshes that allowed human culture to flourish where crocodiles once had reigned. They devised a calendar more accurate than the one we use today, created their own written language, built temples as graceful as any found on the Acropolis, and pyramids that, in beauty and majesty, surpass the best of Egypt.

Then these magicians performed their most mysterious act, one that has baffled archeologists and philosophers, anthropologists, and poets ever since.

It was an incredible feat of transformation. Like a hoary wizard who flicks his wand and returns to the nest of his mother's womb, this entire culture, this civilization of people who had toiled for centuries to rise up out of the swamps, transported itself back to the time of its ancestors. The Maya abandoned their cities and deserted their monumental pyramids, leaving their brilliantly illustrated books, sophisticated calendars, and architectural secrets to the mercy of the jungle. They returned to the forests.

"How long have human beings walked this earth?" Viejo Itza asked me. Standing in the sunny space that formed a bridge between the dark wall of trees behind us and the shadow of the pyramid in front, the two of us peered up into the morning light at the summit of the great stone monument that had endured the test of gods and men and time.

Viejo in Spanish means "old"; Itza is a Mayan name. It was what they called my companion twenty years ago, when he first came into my life. Now I realized that he could not have been so old then, that the name had been a title of respect for a healer-philosopher, a teacher, a shaman. Perhaps, also, it reflected Mayan humor, *viejo* being a reference to his limp, and to the fact that he relied on a gnarled stick to help him walk.

His appearance had not changed much through the years. His hair showed signs of gray now, but he still wore it tied back in a little ponytail. Except for smile lines around his chocolate eyes, his face was free of wrinkles. His eyes sparkled with the passion for life I remembered so well, a passion for love, storytelling, animals, the forests, and people. He wore the same sandals, or at least the same style; like his loose-fitting pants and tunic, they were made from the off-white fiber of a local plant. Slung across his shoulder was a woven bag that I could have sworn had been carried by him these two decades.

I had to think about his question. I knew I had read the answer, but I am cursed with forgetfulness when it comes to numbers. He poked the tip of his gnarled walking stick into a leaf that had settled in our path. "A million years?" I guessed.

"Good enough." He smiled my way and straightened until his arms and the stick pointed up and forward. From where I stood, they framed the pyramid. He stepped into its shadow. I followed, thankful for the coolness of the shade. "Numbers don't really matter," he continued. "We've survived many catastrophes. According to the legends, we people are in our fifth creation—destroyed four times before." He paused. The air was still, as though nature herself had stopped to listen. "Each time it has been the shapeshifter—what you might call 'sorcerer' or 'prophet'—who led us out of the abyss."

Viejo Itza walked up to the bottom step and started to climb. I remembered the story about his limp.

In his youth he was hired to work with a crew of excavators at an archeological dig. One evening he accepted the challenge of a coworker to race to the top of a pyramid. During the mad dash he slipped and fell; when they found him they believed him dead. A Mayan healer returned his life. After that Viejo Itza was a different being. He learned to read, apprenticed to the healer, and—they say—began to converse with spirits. They referred to him as Sabio, "wise one," and put Viejo before his name.

I struggled behind him, clambering over the unpredictable rocks. Some of them were jagged and sharp as knives while others crumbled and fell away as soon as I touched them. I had the thought that the pyramid was conspiring to keep me off it. At first I dismissed this idea as ridiculous, mere paranoia. But when I recalled past times that I had scaled it with ease, I had to wonder. Something was different. I tried to console myself that sometimes our destiny is to endure hardship so we may reach new plateaus. Hadn't Viejo Itza's fall transformed his life? I shuddered at this and forced myself to slow down, to pick my way more cautiously up those terraced walls.

I gave up trying to keep up with this man who was like a human fly. Despite his age and injured leg, he moved effortlessly. One time I stopped to study him. He appeared to slither, his entire body united with the rock, a serpent who, more than being at home on that ancient pyramid, was part of it. The danger, the fact that there were no railings or ropes, did not deter him. I watched him with the eye of an apprentice, determined to emulate his technique. From time to time he paused and, in the manner of a serpent, surveyed all that was around him. At first I did the same, but soon found that seeing the nearly perpendicular wall to which I clung and the ground far below caused vertigo. I would feel a rush of fear, imagining myself hurtling down and smashing into the hard-packed

The author and his daughter, Jessica (at age three), starting up a Mayan pyramid in the Yucatan. PHOTOGRAPH COURTESY OF WINIFRED PERKINS.

earth below. I glanced overhead, but that was even worse. The cauliflower clouds that from the ground had cushioned the morning light now seemed possessed by frenetic spirits determined to confuse and torment me. They spun diabolically, as though sucked by some unseen power into a vortex. They were determined to pull me in with them.

From above Viejo Itza shouted down words I could not understand.

I flattened myself against the cold wall and slowly raised my head, then lifted a hand to my ear to let him know I had missed the meaning of his message. He made his way back and soon he was at my side.

"Sit here," he said patting the ledge beside me. "Not much further. Let's take a rest."

I sat down, careful to keep my eyes on him, the rock, and anything else that would not remind me of where I was. "Your technique," I muttered, "is remarkable."

He chuckled at this. "Technique is nothing," he said slowly. "Spirit's the secret. Remember I mentioned a while ago about how the sorcerer was the one to save our people whenever we were threatened by extinction?"

"The shapeshifter. I remember."

"This pyramid is a perfect symbol." He looked around, inviting me by example to do the same. I did, but focused only on the things close at hand. "My ancestors created a civilization that was destroying itself. Magnificent pyramids. Splendid works of art. Medicines that prolonged life like never before. This poor land was overburdened and the population was about to consume itself into extinction. Not to mention what all that wealth had done to the spirit of the people. They had everything material, yet they had lost touch with the earth herself. Spirit. The wise ones saw this happening. They taught the people to change into lives that would be more satisfying and enduring."

He stood and with his cane drew a circle around me, the tip of the wood scratching against the stones. "As we continue up, feel your spirit mingle with the pyramid's."

Then he was gone. I remained alone for a moment, the words settling in. As I stood there his voice drifted down to me, something about a hawk. I looked into the heavens. It was a sea of blue; the clouds had vanished from sight. I searched for a bird but there was no movement anywhere.

"Be a hawk," came the words. I stiffened my resolve, forcing my eyes to remain on that great expanse of sky for what seemed an eternity. I lifted one foot and set it down on the pyramid—the rock felt solid. I repeated this with the other. I raised my arms to the heavens; I looked down at the ledge directly in front of me. "One step at a time," I told myself. I thought about the hawk; I imagined the sensation of flying above the world peering down at the pyramid, the two men inching their way up. I felt the sun on my head, and knew I was close to my goal.

When at last I reached the top, I was drenched in sweat. I pulled myself over the lip and lay sprawling on a narrow ledge, the pinnacle. The sun was not high, yet its heat was intense. I shaded my eyes and allowed them to do what I had been resisting—look down. Far below, the vast green jungle swept away like the wings of a parrot. It began to spin. I was overcome with dizziness until I forced my eyes back up to where Viejo Itza sat perched on the stone figure of a jaguar.

"It appears as it did in the time of the ancestors." He smiled at me. He had not even broken a sweat.

I dragged myself to his feet and propped my back against the carved statue, squeezing my body into a ribbon of shade. I felt his hands touch my shoulders. They moved down my back. Massaging my muscles, the fingers were strong as a young warrior's.

"But," he continued, "the world is not the same as then." He pointed at a spot on the horizon, beneath the sun. "The city. Thousands of people. Cars and factories. Poisoned air." His finger moved along the thin green line that could have been the edge of the world. "And there, the toxic river. We have entered a time of cataclysm. Like those other four times, our species is again threatened with extinction."

I thought about another jungle, another man, a moment many years before that had changed my life.

"If we wish to survive," Viejo Itza continued, "we must listen to those who can lead us from the abyss."

"The shapeshifters." It had been his word, that man I met "out of place" in the jungle, all those years ago. The word had shocked me the first time I heard it, coming as it had from a corporate executive and man of the world.

Chapter 2

A Corporate Executive in the Amazon

I first met Knut Thorsen in the Amazon jungle in 1968. It seemed an amazing coincidence that we happened to be in the same place at that time: Sucua, an Ecuadorian town located deep in the rainforest that, despite the verdant landscapes around it, was characterized by a single dull color—the insipid brown of mud.

Sucua boasted two streets. Both led to the Catholic church. Not much more than mud-filled horse troughs, they were bordered by windowless shacks that served as homes and *tiendas*, tiny shops that sold soap, candy, and bottled drinks. Built of hand-hewn vertical boards, they were unpainted, decorated only by splotches of fungus and the ubiquitous brown mud. The people who shuffled along the edges of the streets were *mestizos*, impoverished descendants of Indian and Spanish ancestors who had migrated from the Andes in search of a future modeled after legends of the North American frontier. Instead, they found more poverty; they discovered that after cutting the trees the topsoil eroded away and all they could harvest was a single crop—mud. They survived as best they could by working for the mission or by prostituting themselves to foreigners, who came to exploit oil, mahogany, and gold. If they could save enough money, they opened a tienda.

Occasionally the visitor glimpsed a man or woman who was native to the jungle, a member of the Shuar tribe, notorius for their ferocity in battle and their shrunken-head trophies. They were easily distinguished from the mestizos. It was not just their muscular bodies, their rounded faces that could have been Asiatic, the tribal tattoos etched across their noses, black hair trimmed straight across their foreheads, feathered necklaces and armbands, or the proud way they walked—softly, like forest cats. It was not just their custom of wearing only enough clothes to satisfy the missionaries. The single characteristic that made the Shuar stand out from all the other people in Sucua was their cleanliness. They did not wear mud-splashed rubber boots and filthy trousers. Their bare feet and legs, as well as the men's loincloths and the women's skirts, were immaculate.

Sucua was not an easy place to reach in those days. You had to book passage on an airplane that took off from Cuenca. This Spanish colonial city was nestled in a valley eight thousand feet up in the Andes; it had been built over an ancient fortress where the last Incan king, Atahualpa, was born. Sucua and Cuenca were separated by a high mountain range. The plane, a DC3 that had fought in World War II, could not be trusted to fly over the peaks. Instead it followed a river that wound tortuously through a gorge in the mountains. The pilots were known as "stopwatch jockeys" because, lacking radar, they relied on a stopwatch cemented to the dashboard. Twenty seconds after take-off they were supposed to bank ten degrees to the right, fifty-two seconds later, seven degrees to the left. One of them told me, "Even when you think it's a perfect day, you always use the watch. The weather here changes like a Shuar's moods!"

On the day when I met Knut Thorsen I was just a visitor to Sucua, a Peace Corps volunteer on a short vacation from the place where I was stationed deeper in the jungle. I had come to enjoy Saturday night in what seemed, by comparison to my post, a metropolis.

Several of Sucua's tiendas sold beer. You could carry them down to the mission school where the priest fired up an old diesel generator once a week and showed Hollywood movies. It did not matter that the actors' voices were drowned out by the roar of the generator or that the black-and-white films had been spliced in a thousand places since those days before my birth when Allied troops had been entertained by them as they waited along the shores of England to invade Normandy. What mattered was that those images on the ragged, makeshift screen took you away from the mud. You could forget where you were.

Afterward, the priest stood before the dark screen and admonished us all to attend Mass the next morning.

Fortunately I passed up his invitation. Early Sunday morning I headed for the airstrip. There I found a most peculiar sight: a gringo in a gray pinstriped suit standing stiff as a fountain pen just inside the shade of the lean-to, staring out at the muddy place where the plane was supposed to land. As I approached it occurred to me that this was a first for Sucua, an apparition of things to come. Then I wondered why he had not attended the movie.

I stood back and observed him. Mud covered his black shoes and there were blotches of it caked to his trousers. His hair was cropped short and he was clean-shaven. This, combined with the way he stood, caused me to assume that he was a military man. His arms were folded tightly across his chest; he stared straight into the rainforest on the other side of the airstrip. Or perhaps it was the mestizos he was watching—three of them led steers across the mud and tethered them to stakes beside the ruts made by landing planes. Beyond them, lounging at the edge of the jungle, was a Shuar family: a man and woman and three tiny children, the youngest nestled against the woman's breast.

He did not move as I approached. "Good morning," I said in English.

He spun around as though he had been shot. Then, seeing me, his face lit up in a smile. "Good morning indeed!" He thrust his hand at me. His eyes were a striking blue. "You speak English. How wonderful! My name is Knut Thorsen." By his slight accent, I thought him Scandinavian.

I introduced myself. He did nothing to conceal the relief he felt at meeting me. "My God, I was lost," he admitted. "I thought I could get along with the smitten of Spanish I know. But it doesn't seem to work so well." He glanced around. "Out here." He paused, looking me squarely in the eye. "A Peace Corps volunteer. How remarkable! What great, good fortune for me that you came along. Have you lived here long?"

I explained that I had been stationed in Ecuador for four months. And added, "But not here. I live further in."

"Further into the jungle?" He shook his head in disbelief. "With the Shuar?"

"Yes. There are Shuar."

"Is it true? Are they really headhunters?"

I assured him that the Shuar still shrunk the heads of enemies on occassion, but that customs were changing rapidly. Unable to contain my own curiosity, I blurted out, "What brings a man in a pinstriped suit to Sucua?"

He looked sheepishly at his jacket and trousers. For the first time I noticed that he wore no tie; his pale blue shirt was open at the collar. Beside his feet was a black leather sachel-style suitcase, elegant and simple. "Oh, this suit! I feel the fool." He brushed his hands over it. "But, in honesty, it's all I have with me. There's no room in my bag for the coat, so I must wear it." As he said this, he slowly removed it. "In this heat, I think I'm better off carrying it. Although my wife warns against this; says I'll leave it someplace." He paused as he carefully folded it over his arm. "Why am I here? Well, I work for a consulting firm that does feasibility studies for the World Bank. I've been looking at a potential hydroelectric site on the Paute River."

"The Paute?"

"Yes. It's not too close to here I know, but the same drainage basin. So—a justifiable trip for my expense account. Besides," he smiled, "I wanted to visit an Amazon town, a frontier outpost. I wanted to see Shuar." He nodded in the direction of the family at the edge of the jungle.

The heat was beginning to get to me, along with the fact that I had drunk a lot of beer the night before and had not yet had a cup of coffee. I motioned toward a couple of dilapidated tables in the shade at the rear of the lean-to. "The man will bring us coffee back there. I could use a cup."

He glanced toward the airstrip, a worried expression crossing his face. "Isn't the plane due to arrive any moment now?"

I told him about the stopwatch and the undependable weather. "Once I had to wait a week."

His face was that of a man condemned. "In Cuenca they said it was a daily flight."

"Weather permitting."

His eyes returned to the sky. "Of course. Better late than not at all." With that he turned and led us back to one of the tables.

For the next two hours we talked about ourselves, our backgrounds, and our jobs. He was Norwegian. He had moved to the United States shortly after World War II to attend MIT, where he received degrees in engineering and business administration. He joined a prestigious Boston-based consulting firm, became a partner, and was now senior vice president.

"Despite all the good things in my life," he admitted, "I'd trade places with you in a heartbeat."

"Why?"

"You're young, coming of age in a fascinating world where change will happen rapidly. The survival of our species may well depend on the decisions made by you and your contemporaries." His eyes wandered around the lean-to, out to the airstrip, and back to me. "You personally have the rare opportunity to learn from cultures like the Shuar."

This struck me as odd. My Peace Corps teachers had always spoken of what we could teach the Shuar, not the other way around. Before I could ask him to explain, a shout went up.

"The plane's coming," I told him.

His face lit up; I thought he might leap out of his seat and shout with joy. Then, like everyone else in the lean-to, he concentrated on listening. After a moment he leaned toward me, his mouth nearly touching my ear. "I hear nothing," he whispered.

"The Shuar always hear the plane long before the rest of us."

"Amazing," he said. "I wonder what the medical doctors have to say about that." He paid our bill and we hurried out of the lean-to. As we stepped into the bright sunlight there arose a terrible bellowing. One of the steers collapsed onto the ground. The mestizo hovered over him, his knife flashing repeatedly as his arm rose and fell.

"What the hell is going on?" Knut demanded.

"They're killing the animals." I explained that the procedure was to wait until they were certain the plane would land. Since there was no refrigeration in Sucua, the farmer who butchered prematurely stood to lose a lot of money, possibly the only cash he would see in a year. The men worked frantically to cut off the heads and hooves in order to save weight.

"My god . . ." He was watching intently. "I figured they were waiting for the plane, but this . . . ?" He shrugged. "Seems barbaric, but I suppose that's just my perspective. What happens if the clouds close in?"

"Once the plane lands, it must leave. The pilot's better off taking his chances with storms and mountains than disappointing these farmers."

"Maybe he is. But what about us?"

"You can stay here if you don't like the weather."

He glanced skyward. A black cloud hovered close to the mountains west of where we stood. A silver speck appeared off to the right of the cloud and banked toward us. "Let's do our best to speed things up."

We made our way through the mud. As we approached the ruts of the landing area, we entered a zone where the wet earth had turned dark red from the blood of the animals. The mestizos were shouting at each other; the air smelled of blood and feces. From past experience I knew that I was better off focusing on the plane as it swept in across the jungle. However, I was aware that Knut was watching the men where they worked feverishly at their grizzly tasks.

The old DC3 touched town and bumped along the rough ground. When it reached us it slowly turned around to face back up the airstrip. The backwash from its propellers nearly blew us over. As soon as it stopped, men raced to it. The doors flew open. Bulging burlap sacks were thrown out; wooden crates were handed down and passed along a quickly formed line of men toward the lean-to.

There was little we could do. We simply waited and watched. Then I remembered his comment. I turned to him. "A while ago you said something about learning from the Shuar. That I had a rare opportunity. What did you mean by that?"

He thought for a moment, those intensely blue eyes holding mine. "Our world is changing like never before." He paused to watch four men dash to the plane with two heavy iron chairs.

"For us," I volunteered. Other men were heaving the bloody steer carcasses through the door.

He bent to flick away a glob of mud that clung like a dark beetle to his trousers. "We in our culture, we industrial people, are doing some very strange things." He turned to look at me. "I'm an engineer, here to build a hydroelectric plant. But even I can see that the rest of the world cannot afford to follow our example. How many rivers can we dam? How many cars can we manufacture? How many forests can we cut and pave over with highways? How many people can live in houses like mine? It's foolish to believe this can go on forever. Our way of life is irrational and unsustainable. Young people like you are the hope. Yet you cannot learn from our universities—they're tied to the ideas of the past. You must look elsewhere. To people like the Shuar."

His words caught me off guard. To someone fresh out of business school they sounded radical. I was certain that Congress was not paying me to become educated by headshrinkers.

"It won't be easy," he continued. "Ever hear about men who change shape, use mystical techniques to turn themselves into trees or animals? The shapeshifters . . . Ask your Shuar friends to teach you. Techniques like that may offer the only hope for changing your—our—culture."

A man rushed up to us. "*Senores,* get your luggage. Time to leave! *Vamos rapidito.*"

We hurried to the plane. A stool had been placed below the door to help us climb aboard. Inside, there was just enough light to enable us to find our way to the two iron chairs that had been bolted down behind the cockpit bulkhead. We had to manuever carefully around the dead steers. The floor was slick with blood. As we buckled ourselves in, he reached across the space between our seats and touched my arm. "The corporate world is not an easy one to change. No point in combating it head on. Better to shapeshift into it."

The engines roared. Through the windows, I watched the jungle flash by. We lifted and headed into the mountains.

Chapter 3

The Matter of Energy

I brushed a fly from my leg. It flew in a big circle away from the pyramid, out over the jungle, and returned. I brushed it away again.

"Likes the shade," Viejo Itza mused. "You could move into the sun."

He sat above me on the stone jaguar, reminding me of a hawk perched up there where he could watch the world below. It seemed remarkable that he could climb that pyramid with such ease and sit so casually at its pinnacle, after the terrible fall he had taken. Most people would be emotionally scarred for life, forever fearful of heights.

"What exactly is a shapeshifter?" I asked.

He only smiled.

"I know," I responded, also with a smile. "I have lived and studied with shamans. But I would like to hear it from you. You said before that a shapeshifter is the same as a shaman, sorcerer, or prophet. . . ."

He let out a long sigh. "That's not quite what I said. You might call a shapeshifter by such names. Certainly not all shamans or prophets are shapeshifters."

The fly alighted on my knee. I tried to ignore it. "Shapeshifters are shamans. But some shamans aren't shapeshifters. Shapeshifter, then, is a subset of shaman—or sorcerer or prophet."

He tapped his gnarled stick impatiently against the rock. "Words. Just words to describe something that can't be described."

We sat in silence. I knew he thought my questions frivolous. I wished

I had not asked. "After all, I'm a writer," I said defensively. "Words are tools."

It brought a chuckle. "Look there," he said at last, pointing down into the forest. "Tell me what you see."

Following his finger I peered into the treetops. "Jungle. Foliage."

"Look more closely. There. That brown spot."

I had to rise to my knees to make sure I was looking where he wanted me to. The effort was difficult. As my head came up, the sun struck me in the eyes. The green expanse of forest below seemed to dissolve, fuse with the light, to become a vast river that flowed into the sun itself.

"Now." His voice soothed me. "Look right there."

I leaned into him and sighted down his arm. I had the oddest feeling that I possessed the power to make the land below anything I wanted. "Jungle," I said aloud.

"Yes. Now focus." At the end of his pointing finger was the green carpet of rainforest canopy that stretched from horizon to horizon. Then I noticed something else. A blur of soft brown, ever so tiny, precisely where he pointed. I shielded my eyes from the glare and studied it carefully.

"A dead tree. Or branch."

"And there?" His finger moved to a bright red circle near the top of a tree.

"A flower, probably a bromeliad."

"That." The finger settled on a slim stick not three feet from the knee where the fly had sat.

"A stick."

"Aha," he said. "You just experienced what I couldn't describe: three shapeshifters—the top of a Mayan house, a parrot, and an insect."

As he named them, I looked again. The brown blur continued to look to me exactly as it had before, like dead leaves. The red spot had disappeared. The stick spread its wings and flew away.

"Shapeshifters," he continued, "take many forms. They blend in with their environments. Over time they may cause change."

A passage from *The Pilgrimage*, a book by the Brazilian philosopher Paulo Coelho, came to mind. "I once read a story about a man who had to conquer the devil," I told Viejo Itza. "His adversary took on the form of a savage dog."

"Yes, yes!" His voice rang with excitement. "The devil is an expert at shapeshifting."

"Well this man, the protagonist, the author of the story, heard a voice from a spirit guide named Astrain telling him that he too must transform himself into a dog. He said that we must confront our opponents with the same weapons that are used against us."

"Exactly! And did he do it?"

I had to stop and think. "I believe he did. Yes, now I remember it. He attacked the dog with his teeth and nails. He lunged for the throat, exactly as he had feared the dog would do to him. He became so vicious that he scared a shepherd who happened by. But he defeated the dog."

"Of course—once he learned the art of shapeshifting. He became the dog, the devil, and beat him at his own game." He turned to look out over the trees. "It happens out there all the time. It is one of the instruments of change, one of the most powerful, certainly the most effective. Change that happens through shapeshifting endures."

I sat back down at his feet, my shoulders against the stone jaguar. The shadow had lengthened. I had little difficulty keeping my entire body in it. The rock itself was warm. I felt like a lizard taking on its temperature. I recalled how that passage in *The Pilgrimage* had affected me. It caused me to think about the times I had applied such approaches in my life— "fighting fire with fire"—but it had not occurred to me that this was shapeshifting.

"I told you that we humans are in our fifth creation." Viejo Itza's voice startled me—it seemed huskier than before. But when I peered up at him I saw no change, nothing visible anyway. "One time we were destroyed by water. Like in the Bible. Mayan legends have much in common with what you Christians believe. But the shapeshifters brought us through. In the Bible, Noah built a floating island and saved one pair of every species to ensure their survival."

I reminded him that science has confirmed the fact that humans managed to survive a great flood of frozen water during the Ice Age.

"Imagine if our ancestors had tried to combat the ice! Attacked it with clubs and stone axes. Or if Noah had built dikes instead of an ark!"

It occurred to me that the equivalent of clubs, axes, and dikes would be the way modern science responds to climate changes. I told him so.

"Yes," he agreed, nodding his head sadly. "Today your leaders have lost touch with true power. They think in terms of the physical world only."

I understood that he was referring to the realities shamans describe as existing parallel to the physical or material reality that is the focus of science and commerce. "The world is as you dream it," I said, quoting the title of my latest book.

"It is indeed. This is so because shapeshifting takes off from the dream," he said. "It can transport you into a whole new realm."

I had a feeling he was offering to take me beyond the teachings I had received in the Andes and the Amazon. I asked him to be more specific.

"When you talk about the importance of the dream, you are absolutely right. The dream is everything—the waking dream as well as the sleeping dream, our visions of who we are, where we want to go. It affects all aspects of our lives, whether we admit it or not. Once you understand this, then you're in a position to start moving energy around. That's when shapeshifting begins to happen."

I knew what he meant about the power of the dream influencing the various aspects of our lives: health, career, prosperity, relationships with others—that had been the subject of my book. But the shapeshifting part eluded me. "Viejo Itza, can shapeshifters actually change physical form?"

"Of course."

"Truly take on the appearance of an animal or plant?"

"They do it all the time." He broke into a grin. "You yourself have witnessed it."

Of course, he was right. I had seen Amazon hunters transform themselves into trees, becoming invisible, melting into the forest. I had watched Andean shamans disappear into cliffs, only to reappear seconds later one hundred feet below. I had sat across the fire from a Shuar elder who stood up, walked into the shadows and, suddenly taking on the form of a jaguar, bounded into the forests. Yet I had always rationalized these experiences. I had filed them away alongside the accomplishments of Houdini, regarding them as impressive tricks, magnificent deceptions, feats of great discipline and skill, perhaps utilizing hypnosis and sometimes—especially among the Shuar—other consciousness-altering agents, such as the ayahuasca plant.

"That is where you were wrong," Viejo Itza said, as though he had heard my thoughts. "And you are also mistaken if you think they are merely taking on the appearance of something."

"What then?"

"They become this 'other.'"

"How do they accomplish this?"

He gave me a fatherly smile. "You know very well how they do it. They don't really become this other at all, because all along they were this other. They and it are the same."

I felt rather exasperated by this discussion, and not just a little embarrassed. For several years I had been teaching courses and workshops that emphasize the importance of recognizing our empathetic unity with all things. The concept was very "new age." Intellectually it made sense to me, but now that we were framing it in this context of taking on the physical attributes of a plant or animal I found myself playing the skeptic. Despite all the things I had witnessed, I could not imagine myself truly becoming the cat I shared a home with or the oak tree outside my door. I explained this to him. He only laughed.

"Then it won't happen. You must be able to imagine it in order to do it." He gave me a long look. "You're thinking that this is a sort of cop-out. But I assure you that you will be able to imagine it. And then you will be capable of doing it."

We were both silent as I contemplated the significance of what he said. I had thought about these issues many times. My conclusion had been that by changing our perceptions of ourselves and our social and cultural institutions, we could change our lifestyles. Shapeshifting had very practical implications when applied to bringing out those aspects of ourselves that we most honor in others and want to emphasize in our own lives, or to creating what is commonly referred to as a "paradigm shift." This made complete sense not only to me, but also to those who attended my workshops. Several writers who share the lecture circuit with me contend that modern humans have evolved beyond the need to physically shapeshift; that, while ancient and "primitive" people might well have had such capabilities, technological people no longer need them. Instead, we need to apply the concept to our lifestyles and institutions. "The world is as you dream it" had come to mean that we humans have control over the ways we live; that by altering our individual aspirations and our communal biases, we can also change our personal lives and our communities. However, what I was hearing from Viejo Itza was much more revolutionary.

"It all boils down to a question of energy," he said, interrupting my thoughts. "You see, modern people tend to think in terms of organizations. You give your energy to changing the management of your schools, corporations, or political parties. And when it comes to changing rivers, mountains, plants, and animals, you overpower them by using machines that convert parts of the earth into fuel so that the resulting energy can be used as a sort of technological cudgel. But ancient people—and those who still practice shapeshifting—see energy from a more simple point of view. They know that to create fire you don't have to first build a match factory; the fire is within the wood and all you need to do is rub two sticks together until they shapeshift into fire."

He gently moved one hand back and forth across the other. "Energy. It is everything. We are energy. The earth, those trees down there, this pyramid." He separated his hands and lifted them above his head. "The universe. Energy. That is all there is to it. It's just that ancient people were much closer to their physical world. While a citizen of the United States can understand that he and a social relationship—love partner, family, club—are intensely interrelated, most cannot see that this is also true about them and the physical environment. For ancient people, it went without question." He paused. When I remained silent, he continued. "You believe you can influence your relationship with your wife, daughter, or the direction of a company you own. Therefore, you can. The shapeshifter believes she can influence her relationship with the physical world. Therefore, she can. In both cases, it is only a matter of energy."

"And belief."

"And belief. And one thing more. Intent. You must have the intention of affecting your relationship with your wife. So must the shapeshifter." He cleared his throat. "I use that term loosely, because in fact both are forms of shapeshifting. If we understand that everything is energy, it is easy to understand the importance of intent. How can you influence energy without first intending to do so?"

I had to think about this. "It strikes me that I might."

"Yes. But not without the possibility of disastrous results."

His ideas made sense, yet I continued to have my doubts about my own abilities to actually shapeshift into an oak tree. I decided to drop this until I had more time to ponder it. I asked him what this meant as far as the future was concerned, reminding him that we had been talking about ice ages, floods, axes, and dikes.

"Well . . . ," he spoke slowly, allowing the words to stretch. "Here's a question for you. What is the greatest threat to our survival as a species today?"

"We ourselves."

"That's a switch from the Ice Age."

"Certainly. We may cause a new ice age."

"Who?"

"We humans."

"We Mayans? Your friends in the Amazon?"

I chuckled. "No, of course not."

"Who then?"

"My people. We in the West." But I knew that was not correct. "In the North. The United States, Europe, parts of Asia."

"I see. That doesn't include all the factories in Brazil, Argentina, and Venezuela?"

"Them too."

"What exactly do you mean when you say 'we ourselves' are the greatest threat to the survival of our species?"

I had struggled through this one before. I tried to organize my thoughts, choose the words that would convey what I really wanted to express to him. "Well, it's a concept really, this idea that we can make ourselves happy by producing and consuming more things than our neighbors, that controlling nature, paving over and roofing it in, is an end in itself. You know what I mean—material wealth, commercialism, the whole capitalistic bag that has become the foundation for our economy."

"And whose concept is this?"

"It goes back a long way. To the Greeks and Romans. Even earlier I suppose: the Persians, Chinese, Egyptians. Then, centuries later, came the philosophers of what we call the Age of Enlightenment. And the economists like Adam Smith, Keynes . . ."

"But today. Who is threatening the survival of our species today?"

I stopped and took a deep breath. I looked out across the jungle to where he had pointed earlier—the city with its cars and factories, the poisoned river. I remembered Knut Thorsen's words. As I stared into the pale blue sky I could see images rising above the trees, like phantom men in pinstriped suits. "Investors. Politicians. Business executives. Advertising agencies. Television. The corporations."

"Ah hah! Then it's into these that you must shapeshift!"

I felt a tug of disappointment. "This would be an institutional thing then, not a physical one."

"You mean, not you becoming a jaguar?"

"Exactly."

He chuckled. "We can arrange for you to transform yourself into a jaguar, if that's what you want. But we've been talking about the shapeshifter's role in the survival of communities, cultures, our species. You yourself defined the threat."

When I admitted that he was right, I must have once again shown my disappointment.

"Don't worry," he said reassuringly. "We can do both." He paused then and glanced slowly around, his attention concentrated near our feet.

My eyes followed his along the ledge that formed the top of the pyramid, a floor for the stone jaguar where he sat. I tried to imagine myself as a huge cat, but in my mind I saw a glass skyscraper in the center of a modern city; from it flowed a great sheet of ice that spread over the city and highways until it arrived at a desert, where it stopped. Recognizing the city, I turned to him. "I used to work in those ancient places, where it all began."

He bent down and picked up a stone. After turning it in his hands and appearing to examine it with great interest, he gave it to me.

It was warm from the sun, but there was nothing else about it that struck me as particularly remarkable. It was the size of a robin's egg, roughly oblong, and had a slightly reddish hue. Rounded at one end, it was jagged along the other, as though it had broken off from some larger rock.

"Place it against your stomach," he instructed.

I lifted my shirt and pressed it to my flesh. The warmth felt good.

"Into your belly button."

I rolled it along my abdomen until the rounded end slid into the cavity where my belly button was nestled. An image of my mother immediately came to mind.

"Close your eyes. Feel with your heart."

My mother's young face smiled at me. She had died six months before I left for the Yucatan, at eighty-five, after nearly two months in the hospital, paralyzed by a stroke. I had tried before, but this was the first time I had been able to resurrect an image of her in those days when she had been my vibrant teacher. She looked extremely happy. My attention was drawn to her hands. Like me, she held a stone.

I heard the voices of many of the indigenous people I have worked with over the years telling me, as they had so often, that every person and every thing is tied together, that the spirit of the stone and the spirit of the mountain are inextricably united with my own spirit.

"That stone," he said, "will be your key to shapeshifting."

I opened my eyes. A flood of words poured out of me. I repeated part of a lecture I had recently given in New York City. In it I had cited recent scientific evidence that every atom in our bodies dates back to the Big Bang, the time some fifteen billion years ago when the earth was created, and that no atom remains in any single body for much more than a year. "We truly are all one," I said in conclusion. "And we have participated in many lives."

He shot me a piercing look. "You mentioned that you used to work in ancient places, places 'where it all began.' Please tell me."

Chapter 4

Desert Bedouin and the Shifting Sands

Knut Thorsen and I continued to communicate after he left Ecuador. When my Peace Corps tour of duty ended, he invited me to Boston for a job interview. I walked out of the Amazon and became a management consultant.

My first assignment took me to Iran—the great city of Tehran had become a mecca for development specialists and urban planners. It was the early 1970s. The Shah ruled. He and his advisors were determined to shepherd their country back to the status of world power it had enjoyed during the reigns of Darius and Alexander the Great, three centuries before Christ; they were convinced that modern science held the key. Vast oil reserves promised to finance this miracle.

Brilliant minds and famous names representing many disciplines flocked to Tehran from all over the world. From cafes along the tree-lined avenues that rivaled those in Paris to the open-air markets bordering the desert, the city vibrated with excitement. Among the skyscrapers, museums, and palaces there were also pockets of terrible destitution, people whose lives resembled those of medieval serfs; however, a sense of hope prevailed, a feeling that within a generation all that was bad would be eradicated.

At least, this was the impression imparted by the Iranians who worked with the foreign consultants—those Iranians who spoke English and had graduated from Oxford, Harvard, and Berkeley. As proof that this hope was justified, they pointed to the wonders of modern Iran: an educational network that beamed Ivy League professors to the most remote desert tents through a television system bounced off high-altitude balloons, dozens of spectacular housing projects where Western technology was combined with traditional Persian architecture, water desalinization plants, solar energy projects, ports, airports, and highways.

The most impressive of all was the Flowering Desert Project. The Shah was convinced that, prior to Alexander's reign, the deserts had been fertile plains and lush forests. According to this theory, which was supported by a team of US and European experts, Alexander's armies, as well as those of his enemies, had marched back and forth across the region. Millions of goats and sheep traveled with them. Over time, these animals destroyed the vegetation; with the disappearance of the plants came a reduction in rainfall. Eventually, the entire region reverted to desert.

Recent studies had revealed the amazing fact that the desert soils retained their fertility. The experts agreed that the only element lacking for

The desert of Iran. Photograph by the author.

The ancient ruins of the kingdom of Darius, destroyed by Alexander the Great. Persepolis, Iran. PHOTOGRAPH BY THE AUTHOR.

a complete rehabilitation was water. Hundreds of millions of dollars were being invested to plant and irrigate trees. Computer models projected that once the trees matured, rainfall would return to "normal." The desert would flower. And the experts would become wealthy.

One evening upon returning from a lavish cocktail party, I found a note under my door at the Hotel Intercontinental. I was shocked when I glanced at the signature, for it was from a man named Yamin. Although we had never met, I had been warned about him. "A radical," was how a friend at the Ministry of Planning had described him. "Claims to be a writer, but he's on the Shah's blacklist. He's a communist agitator, a marked man."

In beautifully crafted script, the note invited me to meet Yamin at a certain restaurant, if I was "interested in exploring another side of Iran, one that our king will not acknowledge but which you should feel compelled to investigate, out of moral obligation in addition to the innate curiosity I am assured you possess." I could not resist the temptation to meet this enigmatic figure, but I told no one. My taxi took me to the gate of a high wall surrounding what appeared to be a private home in the posh Northern Hill district. When the door opened, a stunning Iranian woman in a long black gown beautifully embroidered with golden icons greeted me. "Our American guest," she said, bowing. "Welcome. Please follow me."

Entering, I was shocked to discover that the outside wall was not what it appeared to be. Instead of a courtyard we were walking down a dark corridor, illuminated only by a couple of oil lamps hanging from a low ceiling. At the end was a heavy wooden door. She motioned me close to the door and then opened it. The sight inside took my breath away. It was a room that dazzled like the interior of a diamond; for an instant I was blinded by the brilliance. As my eyes adjusted I recognized that the effect was produced by walls inlaid with mother-of-pearl and, here and there, a blue, green, or red stone. The room was lighted by white candles set in ornate bronze chandeliers. There were not more than eight or ten tables. Each was inlaid—like the walls—with gems, mother-of-pearl, and crystal. About half were occupied.

I had not yet recovered my composure when I found that I was shaking hands with a tall, dark-haired man in a tailored navy blue suit. His mustache and smile reminded me of a debonair actor, popular when I was a boy, whose name I could not recall. "I am Yamin. Wonderful to meet you, Mr. Perkins," he said pleasantly. "Thank you. Thank you for interrupting your busy schedule to accept my invitation. I have heard so much about you." His accent was a combination of British and Iranian. After we sat down I asked him how he knew of me, adding "I'm such a minor player in all this."

He shook his head. "Oh, no, Mr. Perkins. You are far too modest. You are a young man, one of the few in that august group of consultants our Shah has assembled. You have not yet, I suspect, completely bought the company line. Perhaps you underestimate the power of your position and that of your country."

I felt awkward, very ill at ease. The fact was that I had joined the Peace Corps in order to avoid the Vietnam draft and was now among this "august group" due to a chance meeting in Sucua, Ecuador. I was modest with good reason and had no illusions about my brilliance or influence. I did manage to ask him what he meant by "the power" of my position.

"I think you know very well that our governments—yours and mine—

are attempting to irrevocably change this country. Your government exercises incredible power—in both subtle and not so subtle ways."

I asked if this irrevocable change was always bad.

He hesitated. "We have a saying that the color of the sand depends on where the observer stands. I am certain your country has its reasons for wanting to transform my culture into something more like your own." He let out a long sigh. "The desert is a symbol. Turning it green is about much more than agriculture."

"So it's the Flowering Desert Project you object to?"

His smile was gentle, yet not without a trace of irony. "As I said, the desert is a symbol. But excuse this interruption. We are here, after all, to eat." With his head he made a bow, a most genteel gesture and one that, like so much about him, seemed to contradict his reputation. "With your permission, I will select for us both. It will be an honor to introduce you to true Persian cuisine." He signaled for the waiter. After ordering he turned back to me. "A question for you, Mr. Perkins, if I might be so bold: What destroyed the cultures of your own native peoples, the Indians?"

"Many things: the white man's greed, our determination to expand geographically, superior weapons . . ."

"Yes. True. All of that. But, more than anything else, did it not come down to a destruction of the environment? Once the forests were gone and the buffalo slaughtered, once the tribes were moved from their homelands onto reservations, did not the very foundation of their cultures collapse? You see, it is the same here. The desert is our environment. The Flowering Desert Project threatens nothing less than the destruction of our entire fabric. How can we allow this to happen?"

"But the idea comes from your people."

He guffawed. "The Shah. He is a puppet of your government, a pawn in the great war of capitalism versus communism. A true Persian would never permit such a thing."

"They say all that region was once fertile."

"Pure, unadulterated fiction. An excuse to alter the environment, to turn it into the shapes they want to see, make it conform to the Great American Prairie model. And ultimately destroy the character of our culture and people."

The food began to arrive. I thought I had sampled Persian cooking before, but nothing I had so far tasted compared with the cheeses, fruits, sauces, and selections of lamb that were offered us. However, Yamin did not allow the meal to interfere with our conversation.

"We are desert people," he told me. "And very proud of our heritage. Without the desert . . . well, take it away from us and we are nothing." He leaned closer to me. "We are still Bedouins at heart. Hundreds of Tehranians take their vacations in the desert. Perhaps you did not know this? It's true. Many of us own tents large enough for the entire family—some of them priceless heirlooms. We spend our vacations living in them."

A memory came to me of the Shah's great ceremonial tent located at Persepolis, the ancient ruins that had been the seat of power for the vast Persian Empire. I told him about my visit there.

Yamin's teeth flashed white. "Oh, yes. Our king claims to descend from Darius and Alexander. That is foolishness, of course. The fact is his ancestors were Bedouin. The ceremonial tent is an apt symbol. Very telling. It says more than he realizes. Why would a man descended from Bedouins want to destroy the desert? A man who claims the Peacock Throne, professes to be 'Shah of Shahs'—the king of kings—in a nation of Bedouins?" He paused and touched the wine goblet the waiter had filled in front of

The Shah's ceremonial tent. Persepolis, Iran. PHOTOGRAPH BY THE AUTHOR.

him. "We—my people—are part of the desert. The people the Shah claims to rule with that iron hand of his are not just *of* the desert. We *are* the desert." Lifting his wine glass, he continued, "I salute you, Mr. Perkins. I am sure you have heard about me—things that might have kept a faint-hearted man away. I am honored by your presence here. I drink to your courage." He swished the wine, lifted the glass slowly to his lips, and took a long sip, which he appeared to savor. "True Persian. Excellent, if I do say so myself! I now would like to tell you a little story. I hope you will forgive me this selfish indulgence."

"It's the reason I came. To hear about another side of Persia, as you put it in your note."

"Quite true." His eyes seemed to take in the entire room, lingering on a particular spot at the center of one of the walls, yet, when I turned to examine it, I could find nothing remarkable about it—nothing, that is to say, more remarkable than every inch of that extraordinary room. "When I was a boy, not more than ten, I accompanied my family into the desert for a week, as I had done every year since my birth. However, this time my father promised to show me something very special. He mentioned that I was now old enough to learn a secret of the desert.

"Early one morning, before the sun had risen, my father and I walked away from our tent. We trekked for hours across the desert. About the time the heat became unbearable and I thought I would die from exhaustion, we arrived at a small oasis. It appeared to rise up out of the sand, a dream of paradise materializing before my astonished eyes. A Bedouin family lived among the tiny clump of desert palms. Their tents were different from our own—simpler, covered with a black canopy. They knew my father and welcomed us with open arms. I slept inside their tent for much of the afternoon. Then, after the evening meal, my father told me to go out into the desert with the Bedouin man. I obeyed. We took our bedrolls, two goatskins filled with water, and nothing else. We walked under a sky that was radiant with stars." He spread his arms. "Like here." It brought a chuckle. "Walked and walked, until I had no idea where we were. Finally, he suggested we rest. We placed our bedrolls on the sand and immediately I fell into a deep sleep.

"I awoke with a start, totally confused. The rising sun lay along the horizon, blinding me. I sat up. Not a sign of the Bedouin man! I jumped

Bedouin tents in the desert of Iran. PHOTOGRAPH BY THE AUTHOR.

to my feet, desperate. I shouted at the top of my lungs. Nothing. I shouted until I grew hoarse. Still not a sound. I began to wander around, searching for a clue to what had happened.

"I found nothing. Not even tracks. The wind had blown every sign of that man away. It was as if he had never existed. I panicked and began running. I ran and ran until I fell into the sand, sobbing, realizing that I had no idea where I was going. I lay there looking up into the hot, endless sky, the blinding sun. For the first time in my young life I confronted death.

"I felt like a worm except more helpless, completely foreign to this place. Then a thought came to me: I pleaded with Allah. When he did not respond, like a worm I burrowed in the sand. Its warmth felt strangely comforting. Finally I pulled myself to my feet and stood there alone. All alone. A sort of calm swept over me. The desert itself grew quiet; the wind ceased. Perhaps Allah had heard me after all. It occurred to me that one of the water skins had been beside me when I awoke. I began to retrace my steps. I grew impatient and started to run again. Then my tracks disappeared, erased by the wind. I scanned the horizon for a sign of the bedrolls, anything . . . but I found only the sand.

"I continued on, hopeless, despairing. My throat burned. I grew dizzy.

It was all I could endure. I gave in and collapsed. I do not know how long I lay there before I opened my eyes. In that moment I spotted the tracks. My own! I had discovered my trail. I felt rejuvenated. I followed them until I saw that they took me in a circle. I became delirious. I heard voices screaming and realized it was me. I sat down.

"The sands blew around me. I thought about them, allowed them to enter my cells, my mind, my dreams. Drowsiness overcame me. I closed my eyes, releasing the fear, opening myself to the desert.

"It was then that I heard a voice. 'The desert is kind once you accept it,' the voice called out. 'Once you learn that you are part of it.' I accepted the voice as Allah's. 'It is never cruel, but may seem that way when you resist it.'

"I opened my eyes. Standing over me was the Bedouin man." Yamin lifted his glass in a toast. I followed. The glasses clinked above the center of the table. "He took me back to my father." He smiled. "The oasis was less than an hour away."

"The Bedouin was there the whole time?"

"Wrapped in his bedroll. Covered by the sand. You see, he truly was the desert. And he had never let me out of his sight."

"Quite an initiation."

"Yes. One I shall never forget. A lesson that changed my life."

"You are fortunate to have had such a teacher."

There was a long pause before he spoke. "I often wonder what the Shah would be like if he had been taught the lesson of the shifting sands."

Chapter 5

Institutional Versus Personal Shapeshifting

"What exactly happened to the Shah?" Viejo Itza asked when I had finished telling my story.

"He was overthrown. We in the United States were told that he was deposed by a Moslem fundamentalist movement led by a fanatic, the Ayatollah Khomeini. But it was much more than that. It was as Yamin had predicted. A huge undercurrent. The Bedouin. The average Iranian. Not long afterward the Shah died—a lonely, bitter man without a country."

"How different it would have been if the Shah had been given Yamin's schooling." Viejo Itza's voice sounded pensive, almost sad. "The lesson of the shifting sands!" He was looking down at his feet, his face in the shadows, so I could not read his expression. "A very telling lesson . . ." He touched the stone jaguar beneath him. "Not unlike what happened here to the Maya."

I asked him to explain.

He looked out across the jungle to where the sun was slowly working its way higher into the heavens. A couple of clouds hung above us, like little parasols over a baby carriage. "You know the story. Before the Spaniards arrived this land was covered with splendid buildings painted in brilliant colors. These ruins are mere skeletons of the opulence that existed in those days. Yet they were just the outward symbols of an inner decadence that ate away at the people. By the time the Spaniards arrived the great cities had long been abandoned. Already they had been reclaimed by the jungle. The Mayan people were still here, as they are today, but they lived deep in the forests." He pointed. "Like that house over there you mistook for a dead branch. The cities had been deserted."

He stood and turned very slowly in a circle, hands facing out at his sides, taking in the land below and around him. "It was the shapeshifters. They understood the malaise, foresaw the cataclysm that would follow if the people continued trying to dominate nature, giving in to materialistic greed. So they led the people out of the cities, back into the jungle." His eyes met mine. "Anthropologists and historians have many theories: devastating wars, famine, floods, droughts . . . but all these were symptoms."

"Similar to today's climate changes—the hole in the ozone layer, receding glaciers . . ."

"Exactly. Symptoms. For the Maya the real problem, the cause of the malaise, was cultural—philosophical, perhaps, is a better way to put it." He sat back down. "The leaders had lost sight of the fact that people are the earth. We are not separate from the environment. We and it are one. The Mayan priests and kings had forgotten this. Their egos were swollen. They convinced themselves that they were gods who, sitting atop great pyramids, could hurl down lightning bolts, drain swamps, build colossal monuments to themselves, roof over nature. Their greed was obsessive."

"Like the Shah's."

"The Flowering Desert Project. How many times will humans make the same mistake?" He lifted his hands, palms up—a supplicating gesture. "Look at your scientists . . . will they never learn? When they suggest that pollution, ozone depletion, and the other problems associated with industrialization can be solved by technology, do they not comprehend the message of history? Why do they refuse to listen to the Bedouin— human beings who lived in the desert for millennia but never tried to 'conquer' it? Don't these scientists see that once the Mayan people followed their shapeshifters back into the forests, the problems ceased? No more wars. Whether the floods and droughts continued we do not know; what we do know is that the people lost their vulnerability as soon as they made a commitment to shapeshift into the environment."

"A thought occurred to me. "The American Revolution, democracy, was a shapeshift."

He peered at me. "Can you expand on that?"

I gave him a summary. First I described the political systems that had evolved in Europe: feudalism, aristocracies, monarchies. I characterized them as based on a handful of people ruling everyone else, a pyramid supported by the authority of an army that enforced the will of the person at the top. The majority had few rights; they were abused, used, forced into servitude. Eventually they became fed up. There were omens and predictions of disaster. Trouble constantly erupted, but it was nothing the soldiers could not handle. The majority always lost out; beaten into submission, they continued to do the work demanded by the aristocracy. Cities grew and the populations became increasingly alienated from nature. There were epidemics, plagues, blights, starvation. Meanwhile, the ruling elite hoarded more and more wealth. They and their priests claimed to be "chosen," declaring that they and they alone had direct communications with God. Then suddenly something exceptional happened. I looked him directly in the eye. "Columbus."

"Exceptional for you, perhaps."

"Every story has two sides. In any case, an escape hatch was opened— what my ancestors called the 'New World.'" These words brought a chuckle from him. I went on to relate how the Old World tried to impose its systems on those who migrated to the Americas, but these people who had braved the ocean were different from their parents. They had dreamed a different dream. And they had met a new breed—forest people who showed them how to live in nature. So they resisted their former masters. They rebelled. Through warfare they learned from the Indians how to blend with nature. While the British troops marched around in flashy red coats and positioned themselves in formal lines out in broad daylight, the colonial militias, dressed in homespun and buckskins the color of their surroundings, hid behind trees and stone fences; they made themselves invisible, becoming inseparable from their environment.

He was watching me intently. I continued. "The colonists developed an alternative form of government. As a model they turned once again to the Indians, especially the Iroquois, a nation composed of five, and later six, tribes. Many of the Founding Fathers of the United States—men like Benjamin Franklin, Thomas Jefferson, George Washington, Thomas Paine—visited indigenous communities in order to better understand their ways. Based on their studies, they arrived at a system of government that has been copied all over the world."

"I hadn't heard that about the Iroquois."

"Yes, but the Founding Fathers neglected one thing. Among the Iroquois, it was a council of women who chose tribal chiefs. In essence, the women elected the captain, a man, to steer the ship. If they didn't like the course he charted, they replaced him. Our Founding Fathers failed to include the women. They didn't allow women the right to vote at all—until this century, over one hundred years after the Constitution was written."

"The most significant—most disastrous—shapeshift in human history."

"Voting?"

He laughed. "Of course not. The shift away from the feminine. This world is basically feminine, you know. It's what allows survival. Not 'survival of the fittest'—that's just a male concept. Survival is all about nurturing, loving, sustaining—the feminine aspects. Without them, where would we be? Our early history was predominantly one that honored these qualities; like your Iroquois, women decided all the important issues. My culture here worshiped the goddess, as did people all over the world—all over *Mother* Earth—until recent history, a few thousand years ago, perhaps a couple of thousand years before Christ. Then a great and terrible shapeshift took place."

"I never saw it that way before."

"How else can you see it? I suppose it was a typical reaction. Typically human, typically male. The ego got in the way of wisdom. What has always amazed me is how it seemed to happen simultaneously in so many places. I was raised Mayan and Catholic. In those days, here in the Yucatan, it was impossible not to be Catholic, not to be taught the doctrine. At a very young age I was struck by the magnitude of that horrible transformation that began so long ago—and the similarities between how it progressed here, in Europe, in Asia, the Middle East, and the Andes. There were always those pockets of sanity, mostly in the deep jungles and forests, where the rule of the feminine prevailed, but male cultures came to dominate."

"You call this a shapeshift?"

"A massive one, almost universal. And, unlike those that had gone before, ultimately self-destructive. The wonderful local markets that were organized around the seasons and rang with the laughter of children became the big commercial enterprises that led to the male-dominated economies of today. It happened in education, politics, religion—all the institutions. Pollution became a virtue, a symbol of maleness, of growth. Money and the obsessive collection of things became sacred. You can trace all of it back to that shapeshift."

"And Christ?"

"A great shaman, a shapeshifter."

"How come he failed?"

"Failed!" He threw back his head and laughed. "He did no such thing. He could see that we had to learn our lesson and that the only way we would do it was through experience. We had to suffer all this luxury, all this materialism, this economic progress, in order to understand what it is we really desire. And Christ lit this fire that has stayed ignited in our hearts. Neither Inquisitions nor wars, famines, and papal decrees could extinguish it." He tapped his chest. "It is here, inside me. And there, inside you. We all feel it from time to time. We know it is there. It keeps us going. We will shapeshift again. In fact, it seems to me that your country almost did that a few moments ago—in historical terms—during that Revolution of yours."

"My country had a rare opportunity to reverse that old male-dominated shape." The thought excited, and dismayed, me. "Today we might be offering the world a very different example if those colonists had really listened to the Iroquois."

We sat in silence for some time. Finally Viejo Itza cleared his throat and continued. "I have a much better understanding now of your country. The framework for your system came from indigenous people who felt their unity with nature. The foundations are based on being close to the land, worshiping the sun, moon, and earth, the whole environment. But every day now you move further away from nature. It has been a trend for two centuries, a trend that extended that old pattern that began before Christ. You had, as you say, the opportunity to reverse it. Yet you didn't."

"Perhaps we can do it now."

"Of course. If the right conditions are met. But let's go back to Yamin for a moment, if you don't mind."

"Not at all."

"What are your feelings about this Bedouin man? Was he a true shapeshifter?"

I was tempted to say "Yes" because I knew that would simplify things. Yet the truth was that when I had heard the story from Yamin, I had assumed that the man who had accompanied Yamin into the desert was a good camouflage trickster, that he had hidden beneath the blanket in a kind of miniature tent around which the sand had drifted, rendering him virtually invisible. I related this to Viejo Itza.

"Is that what Yamin told you?"

"I'm not sure I can recall the exact words he used."

"I remember exactly the ones you attributed to him. 'You see, he truly *was* the desert.' That was how you quoted Yamin."

"I suppose then that's as close to his words as we'll get."

"And I suspect pretty accurate."

"So you believe he was a real shapeshifter, that it was more than a matter of hiding under a blanket?"

"I don't doubt for a moment that he used his bedroll or that it became covered with sand. How long do you think he was there?"

I searched my memory. "I can't be sure. At least all morning. Maybe longer." Hadn't Yamin said something about the sun being directly overhead when he opened his eyes after collapsing? "I don't know," I said finally. "Certainly a long time."

"How would you like to just sit under a blanket in the stifling desert heat, sand swirling around you, half a day or longer—even for a couple of hours?"

"Not much. Sounds pretty nearly impossible. But for a Bedouin . . ."

"Are they different?"

"They know how to live in the desert, I suppose."

"What does that mean?"

"How to survive, fit in . . ." This stopped me. "I see what you mean. So you're saying he actually shapeshifted; he became the desert?"

"It's Yamin who said it."

"Maybe so." Then another thought struck me. "If he in fact did do that, how did he know when to return? How did he know he *could* return?"

"Ah . . . the crucial question. The one that keeps people like you, my friend, from shapeshifting."

"What do you mean? Earlier you promised I'd learn to do it."

"Excuse me. I should have said, 'that *has* kept you from shapeshifting.' "

"Thank you. But I thought you told me that it was a matter of belief and intent."

"Right." He paused. "When you think about shapeshifting, do you have any fears?"

"Yes. That I won't be able to do it."

"Besides that."

"That if I can do it, I won't be able to return to this shape—or won't want to."

"A pretty awesome fear."

"Absolutely."

"That fear is the single greatest factor keeping people from doing it."

"How do I overcome it?"

He let out a long sigh. "In a way you have to shapeshift yourself out of it. But that shapeshift is one of those cultural, institutional ones, and therefore maybe not quite so difficult, not as frightening. You have to accept that you already *are* the same as the thing you're going to shift into—that your separateness is only an illusion. You also must believe that there is no hierarchy, that you as human being are no higher on some evolutionary chart than you as tree or jaguar."

"A tough one in our society."

"High school biology certainly doesn't prepare people to shapeshift. But look at it this way: If you believe a tree is inferior, how can you possibly overcome the fear of being stuck as one? And . . ." He bent down, his face coming close to mine. "It's not uncommon for shapeshifters to get stuck." He stared intently, unblinking, into my eyes. "Many never return. They choose not to."

"My God!"

"This frightens you?" He straightened. "But why? If you can't accept that being a tree is every bit as good as—or better than—being a man, then you probably should never consider shapeshifting. Except the personal aspects and the institutional type. Not cellular shapeshifting."

"I suppose that's the attraction. Those people who say we don't shape-shift physically any more because we are evolved beyond that need have it backward. That's just a cop-out."

"Well, another way to look at it is that if they believe this, then they should not do any cellular, physical shapeshifting—they probably can't, and if they could they'd get themselves into a real mess! Better that they stick to the institutional stuff. Knut Thorsen had it right as far as they're concerned. The key is to shapeshift those who mold the communal dreams."

"Corporations."

He pointed at my hand. "Look into that stone."

I held it out to the sun. The reddish color seemed to have turned brighter. I lifted it close to my face and felt its warmth as it touched my cheek.

"Meditate on it," he said quietly. "Go into it. At the same time, feel it enter your heart. What do you want to have take on a new shape? Remember, shapeshifting is about energy, spirit. Ask questions. Always ask questions."

I closed my eyes, the image of the stone remaining with me. I felt my consciousness focusing, as though it were drifting into the stone. It was a peaceful sensation and at the same time I was aware that a transformation was occurring. The thought came that what I was doing was entirely for me, a moment all to myself, when I could search inside the depths of my most sacred, secret self.

"Sparkles like a crystal cave." I wasn't sure whether the words were Viejo Itza's or had come from my imagination. It did not matter. The stone appeared to open up. It was very bright inside, a splendid, crystal cave.

"What needs to shapeshift?" I asked.

I saw a long line of people, an endless snake of humanity—all sizes and races. It grew larger and I felt as though it would devour me. Superimposed over it was another line, one composed of water, molten metals, food, air. This one shrank—smaller and smaller. "Growing populations and diminishing resources spell disaster," a voice, or thought, said. "This way of life must change."

Suddenly a group of men appeared. Wearing suits and ties, they were seated at a long mahogany boardroom table. In the background, scientists dressed in white frocks hovered over racks of test tubes. The man at the head of the mahogany table rose. "Gentlemen, a giant step forward for humanity . . ." His voice boomed across the room. "This corporation leads the world in harnessing science. And I am pleased to announce that last quarter's profits reached an all-time high. Our brilliant Ph.D.'s," he indicated the white-frocked men behind him, "have performed a miracle. And Wall Street is responding!"

When I opened my eyes, Viejo Itza was staring at me.

I told him that what I had experienced took me back to another incident with Knut Thorsen. It happened during my second visit to Ujung Pandang, a port on Sulawesi, one of the Spice Islands with a colorful history of pirates and treasures, located midway between Borneo and New Guinea. The fabled land of riches sought by Columbus when he accidentally discovered America, Sulawesi is a long way from the bastions of modern US business—literally on the other side of the world. At the time of my second trip there it was still one of the most mysterious places on earth, inhabited by the Bugi, a tribe of people who continue to sail oceangoing schooners, often using them to board and plunder merchant ships. Just a month before my arrival, a Chinese freighter and its twenty-man crew had disappeared off the coast of Borneo. No one in Indonesia had any doubts about its fate!

What struck me during that visit—and returned to haunt me after my meditative journey into the stone—was the image of the corporate executives who had come to Ujung Pandang for a clandestine meeting. Knut, himself a highly paid executive who had been hired to advise that exclusive group of business leaders, raised a haunting question during one of our conversations. Pensively he asked, "Who are the real pirates here?" The question had surprised, even shocked, me then, yet over time I had forgotten it and all its implications. Until now.

Chapter 6

Shapeshifting with Bugimen

The Bugi, who have inhabited the coasts of Sulawesi since before recorded time, are feared as the most bloodthirsty pirates in the world. They so terrified early spice traders that a new word, *bugiman,* was added to European dictionaries.

To this day the Bugi sail in large wooden-hulled schooners with enormous black sails. Called *prahus,* they are made entirely of natural materials—trees, vines, and resins harvested from the forests that stretch back into the mountains of the island's vast and enigmatic interior where the Toraja Taglia and other fiercely independent tribes live. Prahus have no motors, navigational equipment, or modern technology of any kind, yet they sail great distances, sometimes traversing the Indian Ocean, known to sailors as one of the most dangerous bodies of water on our planet. Bugi sailors look much as they did when Sir Francis Drake fled them. They wear batik sarongs, brightly colored turbans, and ornate earrings; long, curving cutlasses hang from the red sashes around their waists.

During my first visit to Sulawesi I became friends with a respected prahu builder and Bugi elder named Buli. A man with long, straight white hair, Buli was stooped, almost a hunchback, and toothless; he never disclosed his age to me. He had learned his art from his grandfather, a famous shipwright who taught him the traditional skills. "Every prahu has a dream," Buli explained. "This dream exists before the ship is built. My grandfather showed me how to enter the dream of the prahu as I begin my work. I see where it will sail, what storms it will encounter. This tells me how to focus my work, the parts of the prahu that need special attention. Everything on our ships comes directly from nature; we use no metals or plastics. Once I understand the dream of the prahu—its future voyages— I journey into nature, into the dreams of the plants I need, and select those that are most suitable for this particular ship."

Buli's grandfather had been killed by the Japanese when they invaded Indonesia during World War II, but the family's work was so famous that in the 1960s Buli was invited to Taiwan to help a boat company manufacture ocean-sailing yachts. They wanted him to use fiberglass and design a standard boat that could be poured from molds. He refused to do such work, describing it as "devil worship." "Everything on my prahus must come from nature," he said.

Buli told me stories about the journeys his prahus had made, some as far away as Madagascar and East Africa. He explained that the navigator enters the soul of a bird, then flies out over the water ahead of the ship all the way to his destination, noting the position of stars, the current, and the wind patterns. When at last he returns, this information is used to plot his course.

On this, my second trip to Ujung Pandang, my boss had joined me. It was a far more important trip than my first, one requiring the presence of a corporate officer.

Knut Thorsen and I stood together at the window of his hotel room, watching the harbor come to life. Below were remnants of the old stone fortifications that had been the scene of untold battles between the Dutch, the Portuguese, the English, and the Bugi. Rusty cannons lay silent beneath the palm trees that had taken root along the crumbling walls— phantoms of yesterday's wars, playgrounds of today's children. Beyond the dormant muzzles, black sails were sliding up the masts of an anchored prahu.

"Never underestimate the power of corporate America, of those men back there." Knut tossed his head in the general direction of the conference room where we were spending most of our time in Sulawesi. We had been contracted to help the government attract multinational companies to Indonesia. It was a delicate assignment because, after World

War II, the country had a reputation as a bloody, war-torn place. Not only had the Dutch been expelled, but Indonesians had endured a terrible civil war; no statistics were considered accurate, but three hundred thousand to one million people had been killed. On the other hand, Indonesia's labor pool was vast—and cheap. Sulawesi had been chosen for our meetings with international corporations due to its remoteness; here on an island that was considered out of the way—even by Indonesian standards—the executives felt invisible from the prying eyes of the world press.

"You heard that oil company president in there?" Knut asked rhetorically. "Never underestimate a man like that." He stood staring out the window at the prahu and the men who raised its sails, and let out a long sigh. "The contrast between those sailors and the folks we've been listening to! Here we are in Ujung Pandang, about as far from Wall Street as you can get—yet we just heard the president of a US oil company tell us that he rules the future of all the Indonesian people!"

I agreed that the executive's speech had seemed highly inappropriate, even though Indonesians had not been present.

"'I'm no innocent bride,'" Knut went on. "I've done my share of dealing. But the greed, the arrogance and selfishness we're seeing here! The disregard for future generations! Can you believe the way they use International Monetary Fund statistics to justify personal and corporate avarice?" He pointed at the prahu. "We call those guys pirates! Who are the real pirates anyway? Some of these executives make Genghis Khan look like an amateur!"

The prahu's sails suddenly exploded with wind. An anchor burst from the water and, dripping tentacles of seaweed, was hauled aboard. The great schooner heeled, pointed into the wind, and began the first of several tacks toward the open ocean.

Knut turned to me. "The symbolism." He placed a hand on my shoulder. He seemed almost vulnerable, not at all himself. "That prahu causes no environmental damage." His words came slowly. His hand still on my shoulder, he turned back to watch the schooner. "No oil spills. No smoke. Not even noise." He paused, ran his fingers through his hair. "Compare that to a supertanker."

"Be careful," I laughed. "You're beginning to sound almost radical."

His look was serious. "You know that I'm a card-carrying Republican, a conservative businessman. But that's not the issue. I have children. I hope to have grandchildren. We simply can't continue to tear up the world in the name of progress. Especially when we see that it doesn't gain us anything." He clasped his hands together, held them at arm's length in front of him, separated them, and moved them slowly apart, taking in the panorama of Ujung Pandang's harbor. "These are poor people, impoverished according to the World Bank's income per capita statistics. But do you think for a moment they're less happy than our own people? Do you think their kids are as likely to become drug addicts, alcoholics, or commit suicide as that oil company president's? As my kids or yours?"

The great prahu tacked into the wind. Its massive black sails went slack for a moment, shuddered, then came around and filled. Turbaned men scurried about the deck, hauling on lines.

"No," I admitted. "Their kids probably see the world in a brighter light than most of ours."

"Sometimes I wish our executives had to take a training program that included spending time with people like the Bugi. Perhaps then they would keep wind in the sails, instead of oil in the boilers." Knut did not take his eyes off the harbor. "Do you know that oil will bring more harm than good to Indonesia?"

I was shocked.

"I've seen it happen time and again," he confided. "Not just oil, but any natural resource that's exploited for export: gold, silver, ivory, mahogany, diamonds, oil . . . Oh, you look at the national statistics and they may show an increase in per capita income. I say 'may' because you might also see the opposite happen—an increase in foreign debt. The government may borrow heavily to build infrastructure. Chances are it will never collect much in the way of taxes from the companies—they usually have franchises that provide for tax holidays until they reach a certain level of profits, a level their accountants will make sure they never reach, at least not on the books the government sees. In any case, even when the national accounts do increase, all the money goes to a handful of wealthy families. They take it out of the country, to US or Swiss banks. The average Indonesian—or Liberian or Nigerian or whoever—sinks lower and lower. Inflation pushes real wages down. Traditional cultures are ruined.

Family values . . . everything goes into decline." He seemed to shake himself, like a boy caught napping. He tore his eyes away from the prahu. They met mine. He smiled self-consciously.

"I'm so struck by the differences in cultures," he said. "The Bugi, the Shuar, where I first met you, our own. For the first time in history we have a single culture that truly dominates the world. What we call western is not that at all. It's everywhere—not just New York, London, Rome. It has swept the world: Sydney, Tokyo, Beijing, Katmandu. Even here. Most of Indonesia's population is part of it—the big cities, like Jakarta. This one we're in, though remote and not really a big city at all, is so inextricably tied to it that we can't escape. Here we are in Ujung Pandang, Sulawesi, meeting with some of the world's most powerful corporate leaders." He lowered his voice. "Robber barons is more like it." He turned back to the window. On the horizon another prahu had appeared. With the wind at its stern it was coming directly for us, its black sails spread out on both sides, full like the wings of a raven. "Then there are the Bugi, the Shuar, and all those other little pockets of—sanity—cultures that value what is truly valuable. I tell you, they understand . . ." His voice trailed off.

We just stood there, he and I, staring through the window. I could not think of anything to say.

"So we have this single culture that dominates the world," he continued with a sigh. "And who runs it? Is it a pharaoh determined to leave great monuments for future generations to remember him by? Or a Thomas Jefferson crafting a philosophy to guide his great grandchildren into democracy? Or even a warrior priest, like Atahualpa, bent on long-term preservation of the empire? No. This culture, ours—yours and mine—is led by a small circle of greedy corporate executives who can't see more than three months beyond their noses, whose every decision is dictated by an obsession to enhance the bottom line. Their high priests are accountants; their ministers of state, attorneys. Their gods are investment bankers. And their myths take the form of quarterly reports. The legacy they leave behind is not one of great pyramids, brilliant ideas, or prosperity for future generations. It is, rather, a ravaged planet: junkyards, burning rivers, and nuclear waste!"

I was both speechless and amazed. This man was a world-renowned consultant. He made a very impressive living off the people he was criticizing. I had always known him for a bit of a maverick—how many others in his position would fly in a DC3 filled with bloody animal carcasses to see a few Shuar? But what I was hearing here seemed more than the words of a maverick.

"How can you continue working for such a group?"

He appeared to be lost in thought. The second prahu, the one that had recently appeared on the horizon, was fast approaching. It had nearly reached the first, which continued to labor toward the open ocean, against the wind.

"I have hope," Knut said, his finger tracing some invisible design on the glass window pane. "I'm an optimist. Every human action is preceded by a thought. Every communal action by a consensus. People put us where we are today. This perception we have, this current paradigm, came from human beings, like you and me. It isn't inherent to our condition. It isn't irreversible."

From where we stood it appeared that the two black-winged schooners were on a collision course.

"These executives were not born with their ideas. They didn't emerge from the womb with daggers in their teeth, dollar signs in their eyes. I don't believe that greed is a natural instinct. They learned it."

One of the prahus disappeared behind the other.

"What is learned can be unlearned. At least by the next generation. And there is nothing I can see to suggest that the corporation is fundamentally flawed. It seems an exquisitely designed institution—at times extremely efficient, even elegant."

When the one reemerged, they both appeared to swerve from their courses, their great hulls dipping into the waves, as if in salute.

"The corporation is a vehicle," he said. "A very powerful one. It can destroy us. Or be our salvation."

They continued on, one entering the harbor, the other sailing for some distant port.

"That's why I'm optimistic."

Chapter 7

The Nature of Ecstasy,
and Dreams Versus Fantasies

"Navigators who become birds, shipbuilders who are one with their materials: it seems that you've been flirting with shapeshifters all your life." Viejo Itza placed both his hands on the edge of the stone jaguar. "Knut is an amazing man. 'The corporation can destroy us, or be our salvation.'"

He stood up. Stretched. "The sun is getting a bit hot." He patted the jaguar tenderly and gave it a long look, then turned and started to move down the steps of the pyramid. As before, I was reminded of a serpent. It struck me that sliding along the stones was the safest and most efficient way to maneuver down a perpendicular and crumbling wall. "Wasn't he the man who told you to learn techniques from the Shuar for turning yourself into trees and animals?"

"That's right. The first time I met him, at the Sucua airstrip, in the Amazon." He sat down on the third step from the top, in the shadow of the pyramid. There was a pregnant pause.

I knew only too well what he was thinking. "Well, no, I didn't. Not then. I did not learn those techniques from the Shuar. I couldn't quite bring myself to do it in my Peace Corps days, fresh out of business school and all."

He nodded his understanding. "Things like shapeshifting grow on you over time. But tell me—what do you think your boss, Knut, was up to? What was he driving at that morning in Indonesia?"

It took a while before any response came to me. "After that day he often talked about corporate power. One time he told me that although we might object to it, capitalism was here to stay. He suggested I 'work with' it. He urged me to learn as much as I could of the corporate world. He said that there was nothing inherently evil about the system, but that each corporation had its own dream and that a sort of collective dream had evolved."

"A dream? He used that word? How interesting! Did he define this collective dream?"

I told Viejo Itza that Knut Thorsen often talked about something he called "competitive consumption." He had recommended a book about it but I had long since forgotten the title. He used to describe corporate executives as being a group of cheerleaders who egged us all on to compete harder at consuming. For me it created an image of a line of men in pinstriped suits with pom poms, waving and shouting at players on a football field, except the players were dressed in evening gowns and tuxedos. Whenever we drove by a mall he would call it "The game." He'd point at a shopper, saying, "There's a good competitor, a true winner. The corporate cheerleaders have us all out there scrambling around the asphalt playing field accumulating as many trinkets as we can. The champion is the person who races through the goalposts pushing the fullest shopping cart."

"I have a feeling your man Knut is a real shapeshifter," Viejo Itza said when I had finished. "Or at least he understands the process very well." His hands reached out of the shadow and caught the sun. "I was very impressed by his reference to the dream. Up 'til then I'd seen him as a keen observer, an insightful philosopher perhaps. But that bit about the dream—that changed my perception of the man. You know what I mean, don't you?"

I nodded. I wanted to hear more from him about this. "Can we talk a little about the relationship between dreams and shapeshifting?"

He brought his hands back inside the shadow and sniffed them as though the sun's fragrance lingered on them like a flower. "There is the obvious. The first step to shapeshifting is understanding the importance of the dream. The shapeshifter must be able to recognize both dreams and fantasies, and be able to separate one from the other. This is part of the intent. We can't understand our intent until we separate these two." He gave me a knowing look. "You follow me?"

"Exactly. Distinguish between the two in order to establish intent. Then turn it, the dream, into reality. I teach this in my workshops."

"And the fantasies?"

I told him one of the most profound things I had learned from Quechua, Shuar, Javanese, and Tibetan teachers while writing my last book: that fantasies must be enjoyed, they serve essential functions. I had learned the importance of honoring them, but not giving them the energy to materialize. "That's the difference," I added. "Dreams are things we want to turn into reality. Fantasies are not. The trouble is, often we have difficulty making the distinction."

"Intent becomes muddled. So the fantasies come true."

"And we find ourselves in deep trouble."

"Wondering why it all happened."

"The plain truth is we gave it the energy to happen because we believed the fantasies were dreams." This brought up a question I had puzzled over. "Viejo Itza, you say that shapeshifting is all about energy. But what about spirit? Where does it fit in?"

"Spirit is energy."

"It is?"

"Energy is everything."

"So, when people say they see spirits, it is the energy they see."

"Naturally."

This led to another question. "How about auras?"

"Also." His eyes held mine. "Which brings us back to shapeshifting. A matter of letting one aura—energy body—slip into another, combine with it."

This was very exciting. "That's what shapeshifting is all about?" He nodded. I felt I had made a major breakthrough in understanding. "That simple!" He smiled in a way that warned me not to jump to conclusions. "If I want to shapeshift into a tree, all I have to do is let my aura slip into the aura of a tree . . ."

"Let's not call it 'aura,' since that is only a manifestation. We're talking here about energy. When you see heat waves, you're not really looking at the energy itself. Auras may mingle without shapeshifting occuring. That happens because the two energy bodies have not joined. But when they do join, the auras become one."

"Okay. All I have to do is let my energy body slip into the tree's energy body."

"Of course if you want to make this happen, first you must be thoroughly familiar with the energy body of a tree. Shapeshifters are above all else excellent observers."

"That makes it tough on modern people, doesn't it?"

"It's true that most people today, around the world, aren't taught much about observing, particularly not the types of things anyone would want to shapeshift into. Interesting point isn't it? Think about what you would want to shapeshift into. How does it relate to modern technology, to the things we've been told to value?" He paused. "In any case, observation is simply a matter of training." He laughed deeply, from his belly.

Now the thoughts—and questions—were coming fast. "You said 'if you want to make this happen.' How else might it happen?"

"What you call reincarnation."

"Yes, past lives. But suppose I do want to make it happen. Can I shapeshift into a jaguar without seeing one? Do I have to be physically close to the thing I want to shapeshift into?"

"Not if you're thoroughly familiar with the jaguar's energy body. It's not as though your energy has to literally slip inside that of another. Your energy field has to change its nature to conform with that of the other. But, remember, 'other' is deceptive, because—as we discussed before—you are one and the same all along. All is energy. Energy has certain characteristics that are fluid."

"Vibrations."

"Call it that if you like. The words aren't important."

I recalled reading somewhere that intergalactic travel would have to be accomplished through energy transfers, not in rocket-style machines or *Star Wars* vehicles. Hollywood aside, anything mechanical—physical—would be too slow. I told him about this theory. He nodded his smiling agreement. "UFOs," I said, "are manifestations of energy."

"How do you think Mayan pyramids were built?"

I looked around at the splendor of the place. I thought about all the brilliant minds laboring to unravel the mysteries of ancient construction—these pyramids, those in Egypt, the great Incan fortresses, Persian temples, Easter Island, the Nazca lines, and on and on—and realized that it all could have been accomplished very simply if the secrets of energy transfer, shapeshifting, were truly understood. The implications were absolutely mind-boggling. Yet I also had this gnawing feeling that I was a long way from understanding how to make my own energy body change.

"A matter of intent," he said, without my having to ask. "And faith."

"Nothing more?"

"Observation. And letting go of the fear. Those things we talked about earlier."

Another thought popped into my head. "What about men and women? I mean, can we also alter our sex? Could I shapeshift into a woman?"

"You have been one before."

"In another life? I believe that. But what about in this life? Could I become a woman?"

"Naturally. Male-ness is an energy characteristic, as is female-ness. A slight difference, that's all. Shapeshifters can move back and forth."

"Transvestites." The word slipped out before I could stop it.

He gave me a serious look. "Interesting you should mention that. It is really an old relic, a symptom of our fears around shapeshifting. Those people could truly change, if they only dared to—and believed deep in their hearts they could."

"And understood the techniques."

"I think some do."

I told him about tribes in Indonesia where transvestites are worshiped as holy people, great shamans.

"Have these tribes," he asked, "been in contact with missionaries?"

"Plenty. Moslems, Christians, Hindus, Evangelists—you name it."

"There you are," he said matter-of-factly.

"Lost their courage."

"The suspicion that they might not return—or the idea that the process is evil—is all it takes. So instead they turn to a watered-down version, adopt the appearance, the mannerisms, of the other sex. The shift is left incomplete. Not so long ago their kind did the real thing. Now they are revered because of a communal memory of the powers their predeccessors once possessed."

"That reminds me, Viejo Itza, that a moment ago you said shapeshifting is a matter of letting one energy body slip into another, combining with it. It sounded a lot like sex."

"Sex in its purest form opens the door for the shapeshifter. It teaches us about ecstasy. Ecstasy comes when we experience our oneness with the universe and when we release all our selfish feelings."

This conjured images of old movies where the couple retires to a cabin in the woods and the camera pans to a sunset over the ocean, waves breaking along the beach. I described this scene to him, adding, "As though those old filmmakers had it right—ecstasy is about more than individual gratification."

"The shapeshifter knows that the ecstasy of orgasm is an entryway. That's why so many traditional cultures ritualize sex and encourage orgasm. Mind you, they make a distinction between intercourse and orgasm. Intercourse is about creating babies. To share the ecstasy of sex, you don't need to have intercourse."

I mentioned to him that many Andean and Amazon cultures set aside specific nights for people to intermix sexually. Husbands and wives are free to select new mates for those nights. In the morning, they all return to their families. I also told him that my own European ancestors had similar customs. "Beltane, a celebration that has become an innocent dance around a Maypole, and Sadie Hawkins—they both came from such traditions."

"I think," he observed wryly, "that every one of us has that in our heritage. It's a recognition of our unity."

I continued by describing a discussion that occurred one night deep in the Amazon. I had taken a group of healers from the United States to the Amazon, to learn from the Shuar shamans. The group included medical doctors, psychiatrists, psychologists, chiropractors, and massage therapists. On this particular night I was sitting by the fire next to a shaman, translating for the group. The shaman asked them to describe what they did. During the conversations he learned that psychologists are prohibited from touching their patients, while massage therapists are not licensed to counsel. The shaman was shocked. "How can either of you do your jobs?" he asked. A little later he was told that massage therapists are not allowed to touch certain parts of their patients' bodies. He was astounded. "Which parts?" he demanded. "Oh, my!" he exclaimed, after he had been informed. "But those are the most important parts to touch— the ones that release the strongest spirits and allow us to journey into ecstasy."

"You would find a similar reaction among Mayan shamans," Viejo Itza observed, "if they were part of such a discussion. Yours is a most peculiar culture. You have an unusual approach to healing—to the human body in general, and to sensuality in particular."

"Perhaps it is why we have so many problems: rape, incest, sexual abuse, those sorts of things." I thought about this. "What happened to cause my culture—so many modern cultures—to deviate so from the old ways, to become so—screwed up?"

He appeared lost in contemplation for a moment, then gave me a serious look. "Religion. Commerce. Politics." He glanced out over the forests below us. "When men decided that the pyramid was the answer, the social pyramid with one specific man or group of men sitting at the top, they knew they had to get rid of ecstasy and shapeshifting. It just didn't fit in with their objectives. Neither did the feminine principle—the nurturing, ecstatic goddess. One of the first things they did was forbid sex, unless it was engaged in specifically to produce babies. This accomplished a couple of things. It linked orgasm to intercourse and virtually slammed the door on this portal into the shapeshifter's world. And it meant that women spent most of their lives pregnant. Pregnancy requires time and energy; in cultures where women are constantly birthing and raising infants, there isn't much opportunity for them to become community leaders. Since prohibitions against nonintercourse sex were difficult to enforce, these male leaders did the next best thing. They established laws requiring marriage before sex—and monogamy."

"Which they themselves tended to ignore."

"When have the leaders ever felt it necessary to obey their own rules?"

"So women were virtually excluded from the power base, and sex outside of wedlock became a sin."

"You got it. As if this weren't enough, laws were introduced that excluded women from any and all positions of authority—in the church, businesses, government, even schools. Historically, women had been leaders in each of these arenas. Suddenly they were out."

"How do you know all this?"

"I have very good teachers."

"Spirit guides."

He chuckled. "All kinds of teachers. You may recall my telling you years ago that after my fall," he touched his lame leg with the tip of his gnarled cane, "I went to school, your kind of school, where I studied history." He raised the cane up high. "A very learned man is this old Mayan sorcerer!"

It was the first time I had ever heard him refer to himself by that title.

"You look surprised by what I just said."

"Why, yes," I stammered. "I . . ." But I could think of nothing to say.

"Shapeshifted into a speechless serpent, have you?" He laughed. From the twinkle in his eye, I was certain he knew my thoughts exactly. "One thing more. In addition to nonreproductive sex, those ruling men outlawed something else that was near and dear to women and ecstasy. Plants. Ones the women had grown in their gardens. Suddenly any plants that had been used to open doors to the ecstatic, unifying experience were prohibited. They too became sinful."

I thought of the Shuar. "Ayahuasca. Peyote."

"Exactly. Any plant that helped stimulate that feeling of oneness and broke through barriers of fear or uncertainty. You see, those men had to set up a system of beliefs that enforced their worldview. This could not be one based on feelings or what we call intuition. It had to be a whole new outlook, a devised perception, one created especially to suit their goals."

"Science. The Age of Reason."

His eyes rested on mine. They appeared tranquil, yet I thought I detected a flicker of emotion.

I let out a yelp. I felt suddenly liberated. And with it came the need to release a sound that seemed to have been bottled up inside for a very long time. Then I looked him in the eye. "That's why we now need techniques like dream change."

He pointed at my hand. "The stone."

I opened my fist and looked at it.

"Before dreaming change, you need to be certain that it is a dream, not a fantasy. I know you teach techniques that turn dreams to realities. That's important. But what about the intent? How do you make sure that it's something you want to have materialize?"

"I tell people that they must be absolutely certain, it needs to come from their hearts."

"Excellent. However, here's another approach. A little shapeshifter's trick. If you'll take a brief journey with me, I'll show you. Here, lean back against the step. Close your eyes. Let yourself relax. That's it. Feel yourself sinking into the earth. Start with your toes. Move up your body. Your ankles, calves, knees. Let your muscles go, feel the bones and flesh sinking into this pyramid and through it into the ground below. Totally relaxed. All the way up to your face and head. Good. Good. Now see in front of you something that might be a dream."

His voice was soothing. Immediately the idea of shapeshifting into a jaguar came to mind. I tried to see it.

"Look at it as a three-dimensional experience, a sort of—what do you call it?—hologram."

"It won't come," I interrupted.

"What won't?" Despite the question, his voice remained calm.

"My dream is to shapeshift into a jaguar. But I can't see it."

"Perhaps you don't know the jaguar's energy field well enough. For now, focus on something simpler. The jaguar can come later. Shapeshifting is fine. Make it into something less complicated, like a ball of pure energy."

As he spoke, it appeared: a soft, golden ball, perhaps the size of a grapefruit. "I see it."

"Look at it from every angle. Move around it." Inexplicably the ball changed from gold to blue and grew in size until its diameter was as large as I am tall. "See the total experience, *feel* it."

I could see myself moving into the energy ball. I was wearing the clothes I had worn all day. I was neither walking nor jumping, but just sort of gliding slowly, peacefully, into it. Yet I was also aware that another aspect of me was still sitting on the pyramid. Both were me. As I approached that globe of energy, my image became blurred. It was as if I were melting into it.

"Now," Viejo Itza's voice droned on. "See the stone. Yes. Let the stone move around the vision you think may be your dream—all around it— touching it gently, brushing against it. Take your time."

I watched the stone do as he had instructed. The blue globe of energy, now with an image of me inside it—invisible, one with it—appeared to enjoy having the stone touch it. This was not obvious in an expressed way, but rather came to me as a feeling. I felt joy and took it to be the sensation the ball itself was feeling.

"When the stone returns to its staring point, ask it if this is a dream or a fantasy."

When I did so, there was no hesitation. I knew the answer. "Dream," I said.

"Feel yourself back here on the pyramid now. When you're ready, open your eyes."

I sat there blinking in the sunlight. My hand was open in my lap, the stone resting in its palm like a tiny kitten. "Magic," I heard myself say. Then I looked up at Viejo Itza.

He nodded. "You could call it that. But before we go any further, let's return to the dream-change techniques you use. You said you learned them from the Shuar, the Quechua, the Javanese and Tibetans. What a combination, especially for a businessman! How did you learn these techniques?

"The first lesson was a terrible one." It made me chuckle looking back, although at the time it had been all too serious. "Total agony. I was fresh out of business school—a young man ready to leap into life. And suddenly I was looking death squarely in the eye."

Chapter 8

Lessons from a Headhunter and an Andean Healer

I was dying. I felt totally alone, abandoned in the depths of the world's largest rainforest living with Shuar who were at war with a neighboring clan. I was doubled over with cramps and had lost thirty-five pounds in five days. My clothes hung off me like rags. I could barely walk from my lean-to to the jungle latrine a few feet away. I was a two-day trek and long bus ride from the nearest medical doctor—two days for a healthy person, an impossibility for me.

At first I had convinced myself that it was a case of indigestion that would soon pass. Then I thought it was the flu. But now, on my sixth day, I knew otherwise. I knew that my worst fears had come true. All my life I had been warned about taking care of myself. My family and schools had hammered into me the importance of good hygiene and diet. But I had chosen to live the Shuar way. I ate their foods and drank their *chicha*, a beer that is made by the women chewing the root of the manioc (cassava) and then spitting it into bowls, where it ferments; my feet and clothes had been soaked for days on end as I walked through the rainforests. I had felt a certain exhilaration in these acts of the defiant rebel. But I had also been torn by pangs of guilt and worry. Now I was paying the price. I knew I was close to death.

I lay in my lean-to and was overcome with self-pity. Waves of anger, fear, and despair swept through me. Why had I not heeded the advice of my family and teachers? I passed in and out of consciousness.

The old Shuar lady who had been taking care of me appeared in the doorway. "It is time," she said.

"I know." I began to cry.

"No, no." She came up and touched my brow. "Not to die. To live." She gently lifted my head. "My husband is here."

He was standing in the doorway, an old man who had taught me to shoot the blowgun. "I saw the anaconda," he said. "He tells me it is not yet your fortune to die. He will use me to heal you."

That night, with the help of their son and his wife, they carried me to their longhouse. It was a typical Shuar home, an oval about fifty by thirty feet, built of split-wood staves placed upright in the ground in a manner that allowed the occupants to see all the jungle around but prevented the outsider from looking in—a reflection of their warrior nature—and roofed with intricately woven palm fronds. The floor was hard-packed dirt, swept clean several times each day. They laid me on a wooden bench next to the fire in the center. The old woman, her son and daughter-in-law, and their nursing infant retired to a corner of the house.

Shuar shaman's lodge. PHOTOGRAPH BY THE AUTHOR.

The old man sat on a stool beside me. He wore a loincloth, and a headband made from yellow and scarlet toucan feathers. His face was painted with vermilion lines that resembled snakes. He was very quiet for what seemed like the longest time. Then his wife brought up another stool and sat beside him. They conversed in gentle, whispered voices. She bent near the fire and I watched her pour something from a gourd into a smaller container, a thimblelike cup that looked to be carved from a nut shell. He took it, spoke a few words into it, and drank it down in a single gulp.

After that the two of them sat silently again for a while, until he began to chant. The old man's voice was unlike any human sound I had ever heard before. It was not just the power of it, but the melody itself. He would begin with extremely high, piercing notes. Gradually moving down a scale that was different from ours, he would end on low, deep, gurgling sounds. Then he would begin all over again. Despite my weak state, I found it exciting—frightening, yet somehow inspirational—and tried to think of words I might use to describe it in the journal I had been keeping. The closest analogy I could come up with was that it started like the song of a thrush, moved down the scale to the gurgle of a rushing river, and ended in the growl of some mighty animal.

Suddenly, he stopped. He and the old lady bent together over the fire. This time he held the tiny cup while she again poured from the gourd. He chanted once again, but softly, into the cup. When he straightened, he leaned toward me.

"Drink this," he said, handing me the cup. I peered into it. In the flickering light I saw that it was filled with a thick orange liquid. "Now. One drink!"

It tasted foul, even worse than the cough syrup I had been given as a child. I nearly gagged.

The two of them howled with laughter at my reaction. "Good," he said. "Now travel with the anaconda. Go into the dream that causes your sickness. Change it. I will be with you."

The room was quiet. Someone pulled at the logs in the fire until it died to a dull glow. The night was dark. Outside the jungle began to stir. I became aware of its sounds—the insects, tree frogs, and in the distance the roar of a jaguar.

The old man resumed his chanting. I felt his voice enter me. It filled me. I could see it like a gigantic orange vine that spread through my body and then out my pores into the room. It wrapped itself around the old woman. Clutching her in its barky tentacles it lifted her into the thatching and pulled her through the roof toward the golden moon. I heard her voice in the distance shouting words that sounded like "Tsunky—hah asta!"

I laughed, struck by the knowledge that I was hallucinating—me, a business school graduate who lived in Boston during the late '60s and never even smoked a joint. I knew now that I had drunk the famous vine brew, ayahuasca, considered by the Shuar to be their greatest teacher, a gift sent to them by Etsáa, the sun. I heard my own laughter echoing through the forest and realized with a rush of joy that it was the first time I had laughed in many days.

I felt the old man's mouth on my stomach. Someone had lifted my shirt. He sucked on my bare stomach and regurgitated loudly. I sat up to watch him. He was wiping worms away from his mouth. I looked at the place where he had vomited. It was crawling with worms and maggots.

Overcome with the urge to vomit, I forced myself to stand, and stag-

Tuntuam, revered Shuar shaman, preparing ayahuasca.
PHOTOGRAPH BY THE AUTHOR.

gered to the doorway. I was sweating profusely, wracked with nausea. I fell to my knees vomiting. Rivers of orange fluid flowed from my mouth. I was astonished at the quantity. The thought flashed through my mind that I had not kept any food in me for days. How could I purge so much when there was nothing there? Then I saw what I was vomiting.

Thousands of maggots, millions, crawled away from the puddle of orange. They fascinated me. A voice from somewhere told me to be appalled. "Disgusting," it shouted. I knew otherwise. It was a false voice. The worms were enjoying their liberty. They did not want to be in me any more than I wanted them there. I vomited some more.

I felt a hand on my shoulder. "You can stand now." It was the old woman. I obeyed. "Look around," she said. "See what is here."

I realized with a start that, despite the darkness of night, I could see the trees and bushes around the longhouse. I had night vision. I had read about this phenomenon but had never before experienced it. A movement caught my eye, a giant snake climbing a palm, an anaconda. I went to it.

The anaconda lifted its head toward me and opened its huge mouth. There were images inside. I peered in. People. I was delighted to see them: my mother and father, a junior high school science teacher who had taught a course on hygiene, a nurse, several medical doctors. They were all gibbering away, instructing me not to get my feet wet, not to eat foods unless I was sure they were properly prepared, to always wash my hands. In unison, they warned me that if I didn't follow the rules of hygiene I would get very sick. "You could die," they admonished in a single voice.

"No," I shouted and tried to run from the anaconda. I stumbled and fell to the ground.

An arm helped me sit up. It was the old man. "Change the dream," he advised.

Immediately the forest floor opened up and a river gushed out of the ground. I lay back into it. I felt its cleansing powers. I knew beyond all doubt that it was taking the amoebas and parasites away, that I was being healed. It made gurgling sounds as it swept around, over, and through me. The gurgling became a chant. The chant turned into words, my grandmother's voice.

"We must all eat a peck of dirt," she said. "Don't be so finicky, Johnny.

Germs don't kill. Perceptions do." I had forgotten her lesson. She had been the only one to scoff at what she called the "false facts of science."

Her voice faded into that of the river. "The earth heals," the river told me. "Do not fear it. Turn to it."

The old man helped me back inside the longhouse. I slept deeply.

The next morning I was completely healed.

Several months later I was in the high Andes visiting an old friend named Maria Quischpe. She is a member of the Quechua linguistic group of indigenous people, whose native lands stretch from southern Colombia down the Andes of Ecuador, Peru, and Bolivia and into northern Chile. Once many independent tribes, they were united under the rule of the Incan Empire. Today, in addition to a common language, they share many spiritual beliefs.

We were sitting on a couple of large stones beside a crystal clear lake, looking across the smooth surface of the water at a ridge of snowcapped volcanoes, less than one hundred miles south of the equator. Maria Quischpe was dressed, as always, in an immaculate white blouse embroidered with delicate flowers, a navy blue straight skirt that reached to her ankles, and open-toed sandals. Her hair was pulled back in a loose bun. Her face was deeply tanned and wrinkled. Like so many Andean natives, she has a wonderful sense of humor. To her most things are sacred, but almost nothing is solemn. There is a feeling surrounding her, a sort of energy that can best be characterized by a single word: joy. She is not a frivolous woman; on the contrary, I think of her as profound. Yet she tempers her wisdom with a levity that is expressed by the sparkle of her eyes, the sound of her voice, and the movements of her body. Maria was not particularly impressed by my Shuar healing. "Of course you were cured. All the shaman had to do was get you to change your dream. The Shuar use several powerful plants to help this process. They are famous for that. But the plants are not at all necessary. I could have healed you without any plants."

"How would you have done it?"

"Like the Shuar, we know that the dream is everything. The way we live is determined by the way we dream. Prosperity, health, success in love, our jobs—they are all controlled by our dreams. Your dream was of sickness. You believed that living the Shuar life, eating their foods, going around wet, not using the soaps your parents had taught you to use, that all these things would make you sick. You saw those worms—parasites and amoebas—enter your stomach every time you took a drink of chicha."

I admitted that she was right. "I'd been conditioned to think that way. And I did."

"You dreamed of sickness. So the sickness came. Anyone could have predicted that. But . . ." She held up a hand. "It is easy to cure such sickness. All you have to do is shapeshift that dream. My people would have used a drum. We would have introduced you to an inner guide who would lead you on a journey not unlike the one you took with the anaconda. You would have seen the worms and been cleansed of them. Very much like the Shuar. Except we would not have given you the plant."

"Are you opposed to such plants?"

"No. They have their places. And their drawbacks."

"Like what?"

"The drawbacks? Well, what if the plants aren't available? Ayahuasca doesn't grow up here in the high Andes. If we want to use those plants, we must haul them all the way from the jungle. And the point is, they're not necessary. Plant energy, plant spirit is wonderful, but often the ones like ayahuasca aren't handy. So why rely on them?"

"Could you yourself have healed me?"

"Of course." She laughed. "Although it would not really be me, any more than it was the Shuar elder. All healing comes from the Great Creator and the powers of Pachamama, Mother Earth." She raised her hand again. "The only thing I would need is your permission, and a promise that you would release the old dream, once you saw what it was." She cocked her head and inspected me, as though reading my aura. "You are well now. But we all can use inner guides. Would you like to get to know one, one who will be with you always?"

I agreed immediately, but was told I had to wait until later in the day. As the sun was setting behind the snowcapped peaks we lay down together, the right side of my body pressed against the left side of hers. "All you need to do is relax," she told me. "I'll take a little journey with one of my guides. We'll meet one of your guides—it could be an animal, a plant, a person—and we'll invite your guide to make contact with you in this world. I'll bring it back here and blow it into your heart. You will feel me doing this. I'll then blow counterbalancing energy into the top of your head to help your guide feel at home."

She did exactly as she had promised. When she blew into my heart I felt a strong female presence. The image of an old lady came to me. Maria helped me sit up and gently blew into the top of my head. Then she described the woman shaman she had retrieved for me. She explained that I should spend a little time every day getting to know my guide. "She will teach you about the power of the dream," she added with a wink.

I worked with that guide and several others who came later, over the years. I spent nearly three years in Ecuador in the Peace Corps, then moved to Boston and went to work for Knut Thorsen. I continued practicing the things Maria Quischpe and the Shuar had taught me. Of course, I told no one that I was doing this. It was part of what I thought of as my secret life; I felt certain that if my employers or clients learned about it, my career would be ruined. I also experienced moments of great doubt—times when my business-school side took over and I could not practice the techniques at all.

Those years were fascinating ones. I traveled all over the world, to every continent. I was making a great deal of money, living the good life. Beautiful women, fast cars, fine wine—I enjoyed them all. I even managed to take vacations among shamanic cultures in the countries where I had been assigned, so my interest and knowledge in shamanism grew, at least intellectually.

Then something happened. It kind of crept up on me, I suppose, beginning about five years after I went to work for Knut. I found my moods changing with increasing frequency. Black depressions sometimes overwhelmed me; anger and a sense of frustration I could not quite define became regular visitors. When I journeyed to my guides I saw that I was growing increasingly concerned about the long-term repercussions of many of the projects I and my staff recommended and helped to develop. Hydroelectric power plants, highways through rainforests, and oil pipelines across deserts might add to gross national product, but they were also wreaking havoc on the environment and traditional cultures. My rational side had resisted the message that intuition was whispering into my subconscious, until my guides helped me confront the source of my dark moods.

In my sixth year of working for him, Knut retired to a small farm in Norway. Although he had always promoted the projects our company profited from, his had been a voice of sanity. He was a man of diverse experiences and complex sensibilities. On the one hand, having been raised during the Great Depression and having fought in World War II, he was an advocate of economic progress and material prosperity. On the other hand, being sensitive to the messages of the indigenous people, he railed against the excesses of corporate power and the wanton destruction of fragile environments. I came to realize that I did not share his dilemma, or the excuses his background offered. What Knut cautiously viewed as progress and prosperity I came to see as a ticket for corporations and their avaricious executives to plunder the rest of humanity and all of nature. For me to continue ignoring the voice of the rainforests, the Andes, the deserts, and my guides was a violation of my conscience, a crime against my own soul.

One night in a small town high in the mountains of West Java, I watched a street-side *wayang,* the traditional shadow-play with puppets representing characters from ancient epics, particularly the Mahabharata and Ramayana. The air was filled with the aroma of clove cigarettes. I was the tallest person in the crowd of onlookers, the only foreigner. The local Javanese people treated me with great courtesy, offering slices of barbecued meat brushed with peanut sauce, and cups of tea. They took immense pride in the skill of their puppet master. Several spoke broken English. They stood around me, encouraging me to practice my very basic Indonesian and helping me understand the lively antics of the puppets. Someone explained that this particular show was highly metaphysical, "An attempt to understand the universe and our role as individuals in it."

At one point a young man tapped me on the shoulder. Although his demeanor was shy, he spoke in English with a Dutch accent and the confidence of a wayang aficionado. "You may watch the puppet or its shadow. If you switch from puppet to shadow or vice versa, right becomes left and left becomes right. The world reverses itself. Everything is in the eye of the beholder. It is all a matter of perspective, perception. Like life itself."

I was struck by his words. It was as though one of the puppets had leaped over the heads of the people between the stage and me and slapped me across the face. Perception . . . perspective . . . That was it! It was perception that made all the difference! I had been taught a particular perspective, the *business school* way of understanding economic development. That night I gained a deep insight into my past education. I realized that it had given me a greedy, selfish perspective, that the business school perception was one that enriched very few people at the expense of many. I also realized that in my heart I knew that it was a shadowy perception, unsustainable and unjust, and that the human species could no longer afford to indulge those who supported such a false dream. I rested in my bed feeling a sense of relief; before drifting off to sleep I silently offered thanks to the wayang and the young man who together had opened the doors to this new way of seeing.

Chapter 9

Shifting the Utility Industry

"So what did you do then?" Viejo Itza asked.

"It was tough. I'd seen the light, as we say, yet I had a hard time getting out of that life. All the money, the gorgeous women . . . I even owned an oceangoing sailing yacht. The works! I had an incredible future ahead of me."

"Were you happy?"

"You hit the nail on the head. I was miserable—except when I led my secret life."

"Ah . . ." He turned and pointed at a cloud that had materialized low along the horizon, just above the top of the forest canopy. "Your secret life, where you learned about energy bodies, like that little cloud over there."

I watched it and admitted that my times with shamanic cultures had been the most instrumental in my life.

"What about your work with your own guides?" he asked.

"I think of them and the shamanic cultures as much the same."

"Do you?"

I explained that sometimes I could barely differentiate between the psychonavigational work I did and the time I spent in the "real world" of the shamans. It occurred to me that this was exactly his point. All of it was energy. On one level, there was no difference at all. As a culture we had defined a difference, but it was simply a matter of perception—or perspective, as that young man in Java had said. It did not surprise me when he nodded his head in agreement.

"And your job?"

"I quit. In my tenth year."

"You followed the advice from your guides. After that?"

"Well suddenly I found myself without income. I was scared."

A gnawing anxiety stopped me from continuing. I realized that I was being less than truthful about this. I had not been scared. For months I had suspected I would change my life. I confessed to him that I had prepared a path to follow after resigning, and had set myself up with a private consulting job.

There was silence. I turned away from the cloud and allowed my eyes to roam across the jungle, painfully aware that he wanted to know what this new job had been, and that I was very reluctant to tell him.

"Another secret life?" he queried at last.

"Not so secret, just kind of—embarrassing."

"That's okay. You don't need to tell me."

"But I sort of want to." A huge bird circled overhead. "Buzzard?"

"Yes," he answered, without taking his eyes off me.

"I became an expert witness for a New Hampshire power company at their hearings before the Public Service Commission to get the Seabrook nuclear power plant approved."

"Oh?"

"My job was to prove that nuclear energy in general and Seabrook in particular were superior to alternative technologies like wind, solar, and cogeneration."

"Co what?"

"Generation. Cogeneration." Describing it as briefly as I could, I told him that cogeneration was a way to utilize energy twice, or at least for two purposes. For example, an industry might develop a small power plant to supply its own energy; however, it might not always need all the energy its generating plant produces. So it could sell the excess energy to the local utility company. "In those days, the big power companies didn't like that sort of thing."

"I'll bet they felt threatened by it."

"Fought it tooth and claw. They paid consultants like me handsomely to take their side."

I had read every piece of literature available that argued against alternative technologies. I sat in that expert witness chair and rambled on and on, under oath, about the benefits of nuclear power. My opponents were the Union of Concerned Scientists and every environmental group that took a stand against the monster of a plant that the utility wanted to build on the New Hampshire coastline. I was aware of the tremendous controversy, of the evidence against nuclear energy and nuclear waste. In my heart I think I too believed that its construction would be horribly destructive and that once it started operating it would threaten every living creature within hundreds of miles.

"Why did you continue at this job?"

"It offered money, security." I paused and let out a long breath that seemed to empty my soul. "Somehow I had come to identify who I was with my job. Once I left the consulting company, I needed to redefine myself. Without a job, credentials, I would have lost my identity."

"Do you believe that?"

I had to consider this. "I certainly did then. I don't think I do now."

"Energy," he said. "Beliefs are energy. So are perceptions."

"Now, wait a minute! I'm not sure I follow that."

"What else are they? What are thoughts?"

His questions reminded me of ones I am sometimes asked during my psychonavigation workshops. I teach techniques like the retrieval Maria Quischpe had performed when she breathed the old lady spirit-guide into me. Participants do this with each other. Afterward, someone may wonder whether the experience was real. "How do I know I wasn't simply imagining?" he asks. In response, I ask my own question: "What is imagination? Isn't it a voice from within—a spirit? God?"

"I see what you mean," I confessed. "Everything is energy."

"And what you wanted to do was shapeshift into a new perception, a new energy field around the idea of you—who you are."

"I suppose. . . ."

I could not help but wonder if this was truly the same thing as what I considered a shapeshift, a physical transformation into a plant or animal.

"Of course it is," he answered, without my having verbalized the question. "At the most basic level. Both are shifts in the energy body. One is manifest on the thought level. It then becomes attitudinal, finally changing a person's character, actions—ultimately just about everything, including appearance. The other is manifest more suddenly on the physical level, completely altering a person's appearance and habits, even gender and species. However, in both cases the shift must start with the thought, the dream, the intent. You know, we can't accomplish anything without first perceiving that we can do it." He reached down with his right hand and patted the stone. "I can't touch this rock until I first visualize doing it. The thought must enter my mind in order for the action to occur. I must have the dream, the intent, first. I must believe that I can do it. There are people in this world classified as 'crazy' simply because they perceive things differently from the rest of us. Some of them are physically handicapped only because they don't believe they can do certain things." He lifted his hand. "If I really don't believe I can touch this rock, then it becomes a physical impossibility."

I thought of all the sports analogies, the athletes who broke records because they *knew* they could. An image came to mind of Master Lee, my Korean martial arts instructor, as he stood before a thick slab of concrete and explained that it was his mind that would empower his hand to break it, rather than the strength of his muscles. It occurred to me that this was also true of successful executives, politicians, musicians, and others who dared to break through barriers that often seemed to be physical but were in fact erected by our perceptions, our thoughts of what was possible.

"But let's get back to you, my friend. Please continue with your nuclear power plant story."

I told Viejo Itza how day after day I sat in the expert witness chair before the Public Service Commission, grilled by attorneys who represented various environmental organizations. I often felt that it was I who was on trial rather than Seabrook or the utility company. In the evening I retired to my hotel room to immerse myself in the reams of technical reports that were stacked in cardboard filing boxes along one wall. I was a man under siege. I ate little and slept even less. When I was not testifying I was either cramming for my next encounter, strategizing with corporate officers and attorneys, or sitting in the hearing room listening to one of our opponents. During the times when an adversarial expert witness was under attack from one of our attorneys, I was expected to feed incriminating questions to our side. I took a certain delight in formulating misleading questions or ones I knew my opponent could not answer. Sometimes I was able to discover his Achilles' heel, an issue that dug so deep into the heart of his ego it sent him into a rage there on the witness stand, before those black-robed commissioners. The game of expert witnesses is about character assassination as much as anything. If you can bring another witness to the verge of a nervous breakdown, you have accomplished more than you can ever gain through disproving the technical logic behind his case. The PSC commissioners are not engineers or economists; they are either elected by the people or appointed by the governor. In either case, they are politicians. Scientific fact is less important than the perception that the witness on the stand is competent, and confident in his competence.

"Believes in himself," Viejo Itza interrupted.

"Exactly."

"A shapeshifter, a mover of energy."

I admitted that he was correct, but that it had not occurred to me to think that way at the time. "I suppose," I added, "that I would make a much better expert witness now."

"Please continue with your story, John. I find it fascinating."

"Unfortunately, the more I read, the more I began to doubt the validity of my own arguments." I described how the literature was changing at that time. Increasingly the evidence indicated that many alternative forms of energy were technologically superior to nuclear, and more economical. At the same time, the balance was beginning to shift away from the old theory that nuclear power was safe. Serious questions were being raised about the validity of backup systems, the training of operators, the human tendency to make mistakes, equipment fatigue, and the inadequacy of nuclear waste disposal. "Little by little, I personally became very uncomfortable with the position I was expected to take—was paid to take, under oath, in what amounted to a court of law."

I stopped to catch my breath. Our eyes met. He said nothing. "It was tough," I confided. "Very tough." His eyes showed me the sympathy he felt. "Well, one day, I'd had enough."

It was a day in late February. The ground was covered in freshly fallen snow. It was the morning following a sleepless night but, unlike previous nights, on this one I had not opened a book or report. Instead I passed the entire night at my window, watching the snow swirl around a street lamp. I thought about my childhood in the New Hampshire woods. I recalled the stories my mother used to tell me about two distant relatives, Ethan Allen and Tom Paine, men who fought against the oppression of unjust authority. I remembered my friends in the Amazon and Andes and the ones like Knut and Buli, the Bugi boatbuilder who had refused to design fiberglass yachts despite the promise of personal rewards. Standing there at my window, I dreamed.

Before sunrise I drove to a café and ordered a plate of steaming pancakes with real New Hampshire maple syrup. It was a breakfast I had always loved, a pleasure I had not indulged in for months. The realization of the sacrifice I had made—was making—struck me every bit as hard as if one of those maple trees had fallen on me. As I left the café and slid into the seat of my rental car, I was overcome by a sort of dizziness. I closed my eyes. The old lady that Maria Quischpe had blown into me appeared. Suddenly everything became clear.

I took the utility company's executive vice president and chief attorney aside before the hearings began and told them I could no longer work for them. They, of course, were shocked. I insisted that in good faith I could no longer defend Seabrook; I asked them whether they expected me to lie under oath. To their credit, they agreed that I should simply "disappear" as an expert witness. "What will you do now?" the executive vice president asked. Without a moment's hesitation I replied, "Start a company to develop cogeneration."

I turned to Viejo Itza. "The idea came to me that quickly. From the old lady."

"And the company?"

"I formed it. It turned out to be a much more difficult job than I ever anticipated. Had I known then all the heartache I would endure over the next nine years, I would never have begun it. The industry was in its pioneer phase. Laws that made the whole business possible were only passed that year, 1982. Actually it was a 1978 law that had been challenged by the utility industry because it was such a threat to them. In

1982 the law was upheld by the Supreme Court. I stepped into a hornet's nest."

"What a shapeshift that was!"

"I guess it was. One of those institutional ones."

"And personal. I'm sure you changed. Even in appearance."

He was right. I became a different person. As an executive I had always been competent, and confident. However, I now actively introduced shamanism into a business that was rooted in the conservative engineering profession and Wall Street. All our planning, all our work, involved psychonavigation. Spirit guides were consulted each time a major decision had to be made. I would sit at a boardroom table in a navy blue pinstriped suit, surrounded by two dozen lawyers and investment bankers, and take a brief journey to my guides. I had become proficient, like my indigenous teachers; I could accomplish this without any visible sign that I was anywhere other than that room. But people close to me knew. Word got around.

In addition to bringing shamanism into the business world, I changed in other ways. My personal life took a drastic turn. I met Winifred and fell deeply in love. We married and I, a man who had sworn that he would never have the time or inclination for a child, found myself transformed into a husband, and then a father. Family life has been one of the most exciting and rewarding adventures of my life.

My company prospered. Of the eighty-four independent power companies registered to develop projects in the states where we worked, only seven were successful. The rest folded. Of those seven, the other six sold out to large engineering construction conglomerates. Mine alone made it on its own. It was also the only one that had a policy of developing energy projects that would serve as models by proving that new, ecologically beneficial technologies were feasible and finance-able. I wanted to see my company make money, but that was not my primary objective.

Once the company was established, I decided to move on. It had been nearly a decade since that snowy morning when I walked out of the Public Service Commission hearing room. By the time I sold my ownership in November 1990, my company had accumulated an impressive record, one that proved what Seabrook opponents had known all along—that cogeneration was superior to nuclear power; it was safer and more economical. We had established ourselves as a leader in developing innovative, environmentally friendly energy projects, including one that had sent the industry into a tailspin. It was a $55 million (in 1986 dollars) power plant that burned waste coal and utilized its cooling system to heat a hydroponic greenhouse. Most important, it was designed around a revolutionary boiler that converted mountains of "nonusable" hazardous coal slag into electricity without producing any acid rain, accomplishing what all the books I had read during those long New Hampshire nights considered impossible. This particular project was cited by the US House of Representatives and written up in the *Congressional Record* as an example of American ingenuity and entrepreneurship.

I had been called a radical. I had been threatened by old friends and taken to court by my former clients, the utility companies. In the end we won every battle. "Now," I told Viejo Itza, "cogeneration has taken the world by storm. And that revolutionary boiler? Today it is classified as 'standard,' a great step forward in eradicating acid rain pollution."

"Extremely impressive," he said. "And you did not consider yourself a shapeshifter?"

"I guess I never thought about it that way."

"You certainly moved a lot of energy." He chuckled. "In many ways."

"I suppose I've always thought of shapeshifters as people who transform themselves into jaguars."

"One form."

"I see that now." I knew I had to speak what was on my mind. "I still would like to try that form, become a jaguar."

"I thought it was a ball of energy you wanted to shapeshift into."

"That will do, for a start. But I must really become it."

"You will. In the meantime, it's important to recognize that what you accomplished with your company and yourself was a shapeshift. Major."

He held me in a long look, then broke into a smile, as though he had some secret he was not quite willing to share. Slowly his eyes left mine and moved high over my head. "Can you believe it! It is already well after noon."

"We've covered a lot here today. You've helped me understand many things. Thank you."

"You're welcome. I've whetted your appetite."

"That too."

He stood up stiffly and stretched. "This rock can get pretty hard." He made his way back up the steps to the stone jaguar. I noticed for the first time that it faced us. It seemed to be studying me. He picked his woven shoulder bag up from where he had left it beside the jaguar's paw and returned to my side.

"Are you hungry, my friend?" he asked, and sat down. He fumbled around in the bag and produced a gourd and a package of banana leaves tied together with a thin vine. He held the gourd out to me; it was a beautiful dark brown color, and had the appearance of a polished statue. He pulled off its top. "Remember our conversation about sex? How it can open the door for the shapeshifter, teaching about the ecstatic unity we feel when we release our selfish feelings and experience our oneness with the universe? This gourd is a good symbol. People are like gourds; to get to the good stuff inside, we must lift off our tops. Sex—and teacher plants, like ayahuasca—can help open us up. Sometimes."

He handed it to me. I lifted it to my lips. The liquid inside reminded me a little of the Shuars' chicha. It definitely had a kick. Next, he unwrapped the package of banana leaves. Inside was a stack of tortillas. We ate in silence.

"You described dream experiences with the Shuar and Quechua. You also mentioned something about Java and Tibet. How do they fit in?"

Chapter 10

Transition

We drove into the mountains of West Java, Indonesia. My chauffeur/translator worked for the Ministry of Energy; it was obvious that the pride he felt for his people and the land was genuine. The higher into the mountains we went, the more enthusiastic he became. "The gods created this place," he told me, "so we mortals can preview paradise."

He took me into a little village where barefoot boys kicked a ball down the street in front of us as though challenging our jeep to a game. When I leaned through the open window to snap photographs, one of them picked up the ball and, standing with his arms and legs akimbo, shouted in heavily accented English, "My name John Wayne."

After leaving them, I commented to the driver that the boys looked skinny and poor.

"I'm Javanese," he said puffing up his chest. "I grew up near here, like them. Those boys may not have money, but they're not poor. I know." He paused and continued to drive. "It is only your perception of wealth." He swept his hand across the windshield. "How can anyone who has all this be poor?" He glanced my way. "We Javanese are very aware of the tricks perceptions can play."

His words took me back to that night at the shadow-play. I repeated for him the wisdom of the young man who had spoken to me about perspective, and the way his philosophy had affected me.

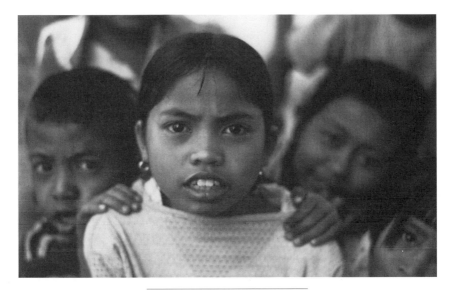

Javanese children. PHOTOGRAPH BY THE AUTHOR.

"Yes, yes," he said with a chuckle. "You are learning from us. You see?"

I asked him whether he was familiar with the idea of shapeshifting.

"What Javanese is not? It is part of life here. You know, we have a saying that all is illusion."

"We too say something like that. Except we put it a little differently. We say 'Nothing is real except death and taxes.'"

He laughed. "We Javanese might agree to the part about taxes, but not death." He gave me a long look before turning back to the road. "What is real about death? It is just another shapeshift, one each of us learns to do."

This stunned me for an instant. "What a concept!"

"That death is an illusion?"

"No, that it is a shapeshift each of us learns to do." I could not get over the simplicity and the profundity of that statement. "Do you truly believe this?"

"Of course. Death does not exist. We pass on, that's all—take a new form. Reincarnation. It is the essence of shapeshifting. It comes easily for those of us who know it is merely a transformation into a new form. I always feel sorry for people who don't believe this. Death comes painfully for them—their own and the death of loved ones."

Javanese mother and child. PHOTOGRAPH BY THE AUTHOR.

I thought back to people I knew who had died. Most fought it to the end, their families and doctors encouraging, even begging, them to stay alive. How different from stories I had read about the Buddha and others who believed in reincarnation! How different from the shamans! "I like that," I said.

It brought a smile. "Of course you do. Whether we are right or not—I know we are, but you may disagree—it's certainly a much happier way to live."

"And die."

"Absolutely."

I kept thinking about this as we drove deeper into the mountains. It fascinated me to consider that, in a culture like mine where materialism ruled and people tended not to believe in things like shapeshifting, ultimately every one of us did it anyway. Even if you did not believe in it, if reincarnation were a fallacy, still every single person shapeshifted. Could any rational person deny that the human being was totally transformed by death? It did not require a belief in spirituality to admit that the body shifted into something else. Shakespeare's scene where Hamlet peers at Yorick's skull and philosophizes about a man dying, being buried, and turning to earth and worms summed up a materialist's—or a scientist's—

point of view pretty accurately. It also described an undeniable shapeshift. I was struck again by the magnitude of this concept—that every one of us shapeshifts, whether we believe in it or not.

I discussed this with my driver. He pulled a pen from his shirt pocket and dropped it on the seat beside me. "What happened?" he asked. Without waiting for my answer, he responded, "Gravity caused my pen to fall. Am I right? Yes, of course. We all know that. Every educated, reasonable person on this planet would agree. Right? But what if someone didn't agree? What if there were people who never heard of gravity? What if we lived at the time of the cavemen? Or if there were no people, just animals who had no idea whatsoever about gravity. Well, my pen—or a tree branch—would fall just the same. Gravity would cause it to fall whether anyone understood this concept or not. The same is true of shapeshifting. It happens. We all end up doing it. Many, many times. If you believe in reincarnation, we do it at least once every lifetime."

Soon after that we reached the city of Bandung. My driver drove us directly to the government guest house where I would live for the next three months. Built during the Dutch colonial period, its spacious veranda faced tea plantations that spread across the rolling hills and up the slopes of mountains that, when we arrived, were slowly fading into the purple shadows of evening.

An old man trotted down the steps; his loose-fitting pants flapped about his sandals. He wore a batik shirt that flowered in vibrant colors with the hero-gods of ancient Javanese mythology.

"A true shapeshifter," my driver mused as he approached.

I climbed out of the jeep, brushing the road dust from my jeans, and held out my hand. He grinned sheepishly. Then touching his fingers together over his heart, he bowed. "Me Toyup," he said in a cackling voice.

Toyup and I spent many hours together. He taught me a great deal, some of which is described in my first book, *The Stress-Free Habit*. He was indeed a shapeshifter, yet he stated it somewhat differently. *"Be"* he would say, his face breaking into a toothless grin. "Always *be*. Never try to *become*. You can *be* anything you want, just don't work at *becoming*. Remember to *be* it."

At first I found this rather confusing, but he kept at me with perseverance and patience. Several times he told me different versions of the same

Government guest house in West Java. PHOTOGRAPH BY THE AUTHOR.

story. This story, called "O-Nami" (Great Waves), is included in *The Stress-Free Habit;* it inspired many people to write to me. I repeat the story here.

O-Nami was a well-known wrestler of superb strength and fighting knowledge. He could defeat anyone, even his instructor, as long as he fought in private. Public appearances, though, were a different matter. He became self-conscious and unsure of himself. He made foolish mistakes and often lost to wrestlers of inferior ability.

One night a master instructor visited him. The master was reputed to be one of the wisest. "O-Nami," he said, "You are the Great Waves. You must believe it. Be it. Go to your room. Stay awake the night through and think about Great Waves. Believe in what you are. You are those gigantic swells that destroy everything in their path."

O-Nami retired to his room. All night long he meditated. At first he merely thought about waves. Other visions intruded, but he brushed them aside. Gradually, as the night wore on, the waves took over. They filled the room, rushing and swirling over him. When the sun rose on O-Nami's room, it was a flood of thundering waves.

After that, no one was able to defeat O-Nami.

"People in the audience swore they saw O-Nami roll over his opponents like a breaking wave," Toyup told me. "Other wrestlers accused him of sucking out their breath—what they described was defeat by drowning!"

Toyup loved that story. "It gets to the heart of the matter," he would say. "You talk about shapeshifting. Bah! It is simply a matter of *being*. We can be anything, because in fact we are all things. Each of us is everything else; there is no everything else."

He used to tell me many stories about people who were always seeking to become, rather than simply being; one story about a Balinese dancer who was the daughter of an old friend exemplifies them all. This young woman studied dance day in and day out. "I am going to become a dancer," she would say. After several years of continuous practice she grew discouraged. Her father sent her to Toyup.

"I go to auditions, but I am never quite ready," she told him. "I am determined to become a dancer—if only I could just land my first job."

"Determined to become a dancer? But, don't you dance every day?"

"Of course. I practice constantly."

"You dance?'

"All the time."

"Then you are a dancer." He asked to see a demonstration. Afterward he told her that it was the most beautiful performance he had ever seen. He repeated, "You are a dancer."

"But I've never been hired to perform."

"So? Because some foolish dance master hasn't yet hired you is irrelevant. If one were to hire you tomorrow, would you be a better dancer than you were tonight?" She shook her head. "Right. You would be the same: a great dancer. You are a dancer. Be one."

Within a week she had been hired by the most important dance company in Jakarta.

Late one afternoon Toyup asked me to meet him in a grove of trees not far from the guest house where we lived. "Give me a half hour," he said. "Then come to where the log bench is. I have something to show you."

I waited eagerly for that half hour to pass. At the time I was reading Hermann Hesse's *Siddhartha;* I had great difficulty concentrating on the book. I had a feeling that something important was about to happen.

Finally the time arrived. I could barely hold myself back; I almost ran to the grove of trees. When I got there I slowed to a dignified walk, trying to imitate Toyup's casual manner, not wanting him to witness my impatience. I strolled up to the log bench and glanced around. There was no sign of him. I walked in a circle around the grove looking everywhere, but Toyup was not to be found. Disappointed and frustrated, I decided to wait a few minutes. I sat down on the bench.

After a while I began to feel drowsy. I lay down on the bench and closed my eyes. The breeze rustled the leaves around me, soothing me. I must have dozed off. Then something touched my cheek. I sat up and looked. There was a stubby, leafless bush behind my bench that looked almost dead. I theorized that one of its branches had brushed against me. I lay back down and had just begun to doze off again when I felt the branch touch the top of my head. I grabbed it. A hand! I sat up and saw Toyup. He was crouching behind my bench in the process of transforming himself from that bush to an old Javanese man, himself. I could not believe my eyes. He was stark naked.

I jumped up and stood beside him. "How did you do that?" I demanded.

He walked stiffly to another tree and pulled a little satchel from a hole under its roots. He took out his shirt, trousers, and sandals and put them on. Then he started back toward me. "Do what?"

"You know. Become that bush."

He stood very close to me, staring directly into my eyes, something he had seldom done before. "Have you learned nothing?" he asked, and I could detect genuine disappointment in his voice. "I did not become that tree. Anymore than I now have become an old Javanese man."

It stopped me. "You are you, are being you. You were the tree."

He allowed a smile. "That's right."

"But how?"

"The same way you are the you I see here before me."

Another question gnawed at me. I was reluctant to ask him, yet knew I must. "Why did you take off your clothes?"

"Colors," he said slowly, "seem to have energies that vibrate on their own. I have difficulty wearing clothes of one color and being something that is another color."

We sat down on the bench together. "I think O-Nami was able to overcome this color thing. But I have not yet unlocked that door."

I apologized for asking foolish questions and missing his point about being.

"These things take time," he said softly. "Be patient. I know you want to do what I just did and I know you will. But you're not ready just yet." His eyes conveyed deep compassion. "Be thankful for what you've experienced."

I turned and hugged him. I could not help myself. "I am," I blurted out. Then I began to sob uncontrollably.

"Toyup introduced me to a beautiful young Italian woman, Marina Bellazzi," I said to Viejo Itza. "She was traveling around Asia."

As he nibbled at a tortilla and washed it down with the fermented drink, I told him how she and I had become friends, eventually coleading a group of Italians and North Americans to the Shuar. Marina was a talented artist whose paintings were deeply influenced by her experiences in Tibet. She had lived in the Himalayas and had devoted much of her life to studying Tibetan customs, rituals, and healing techniques. Her masters were Tibetan shamans. She taught me a dream-changing technique she had learned from them. I shared it with Viejo Itza as the following eight-step approach.

"First, select a dream, something you know from the depths of your soul you want to have come true. You could take that journey you taught me, using the stone to distinguish dreams from fantasies. . . .

"Second, with eyes closed see a very black place, a sort of void. A silver star appears, surrounded by the blackness. Send your dream out to the star. Watch the star absorb the dream. . . .

"Third, bring the star (with the dream) into your forehead, allowing it to pass through your third eye, between and slightly above your two eyes. . . .

"Fourth, envision the inside of your head as a crystal ball or a globe of mirrors. The dream and star are now reflected and magnified throughout this splendid place. . . .

"Fifth, watch the dream and star explode three times. Each time, instead of being destroyed, they are energized. They become thoroughly integrated with your mind. . . .

t them drop down into your heart. See it also as a place lined
where dream and star are magnified. . . .

Seventh, watch the dream and star explode three times. With each
explosion, reaffirm your commitment to making this dream become a
reality. Feel the energy of your heart and the fusion that takes place between your heart, the dream, and the star. . . .

"Eighth, let them rise up through your head, out the third eye, and
back into the blackness."

I glanced up and caught Viejo Itza with his eyes closed. Slowly, he
opened them. "Powerful" was all he said.

Marina stressed the importance of repeating that exercise at least three
times a week—more if I felt so inclined.

I described ways I had adapted this technique for use in my workshops. "I tell participants, 'Since you want your dream to come true in
this ordinary reality, you need to take the process a step further. Give
energy to your dream every day by doing something concrete that directly helps your dream materialize. Write letters, call politicians. Do
something. Also give voice to your dream. Talk about it. Verbalize it."

"The word," he said, rolling the sound on his tongue. "Every culture
recognizes the importance of verbalizing the dream, or proclaiming it
symbolically."

I agreed, adding, "Expressing our dream to others seems to be uni-
versally recognized as having great power. Except perhaps in modern
industrial-technological societies like mine."

He looked at me for a long time without speaking. His eyes just seemed
to hold me—not to study or explore, but simply to envelop me. Finally,
after what seemed an eternity, he blinked. "It is time for you to go," he
said.

"To go?"

"Back to your friends the Shuar deep in the forest." He smiled. "Take
others with you. Share this power of the dream and the word. Build the
energy. You have entered a very important moment. The transition. Do
not waste it. Have faith. Learn to shapeshift in all its forms."

Part 2

THE
VIEW
FROM
WITHIN

Chapter 11

An Amazon Shaman Disappears

Deep in the Amazon rainforest, the stars possessed the night. As I stepped through the doorway of the shaman's lodge, I was overwhelmed by the tiny spheres of light that swirled about me. They were everywhere. Not just in the heavens above, but also under my feet. I stood very still listening to the sounds of the jungle, watching the fiery ballet.

Beyond the tiny clearing around the shaman's home, the trees were silhouetted by the brilliant lights that danced among them, like millions of tiny angels. It seemed like a perfect night for shapeshifting—a night when stars and fireflies merged, and people, plants, animals, rocks, dreams, and nightmares became one, when subatomic particles absorbed the universe. It was a night I shared with a group of North American scientists, doctors, psychologists, and teachers I had brought to Ecuador to work with the shamans.

Viejo Itza had planted the seed. Once I had committed to following his advice, to building little mounds of soil around the seed and watering it, the rest had come with surprising ease. Because of my books and seminars, many people had taken an interest in my work with shamanic cultures. I formed a partnership with two Ecuadorian friends, Raul and Jaime, and spread the word that people who wanted to "change the dream" could visit the Shuar. Together we took small groups of North Americans and Europeans high into the Andes and deep into the jungles. We called our work Dream Change Adventures: Serving Earth Through Self-awareness. The seed sprouted.

After the first couple of trips Jaime committed himself to helping the Achuar, a neighboring tribe that, despite a shared language and cosmology, are traditional enemies of the Shuar. The Achuar had only recently been contacted by missionaries and we all agreed that it would be beneficial for Jaime to work with them. He would explore the possibility of helping them build an ecological lodge where they could teach northerners about sustainable, earth-honoring ways of life. Increasingly he left the trips into Shuar territory up to Raul and me.

On this particular night the two of us had taken a group of fourteen to visit Kitiar, an elder Shuar shaman I had known for years. It was a night when we, the "civilized," experienced things we had never before imagined, when Ph.D.'s sat at the feet of an illiterate man who spoke the language of a small jungle tribe and communicated profound ideas.

Tuntuam performing a greeting dance.
PHOTOGRAPH BY THE AUTHOR.

"Your people must change," he told us. "Your way of seeing the world can not continue. Yet, you are the leaders. The whole world follows your path. You, all of you, must work to change your people from the greedy beast that devours everything to one who learns respect, love." He studied me. "You have asked about shapeshifting. I will show you a shift myself. It is my time to become the bat and fly away." He began to laugh so hard that I feared it would choke him. When he stopped, he held his hands out to include all the people in the group. "I, the bat, will fly away. But you must shift your people. Bring more of them here to learn from my people. Then help them go out and teach others."

That night his chanting was more powerful even than usual. His *tumank*, a single-stringed instrument that looks like a small hunting bow and is played like a mouth harp, created melodies that took us all on journeys.

Once in a while he would stop making music and talk about the forests. "Filled with incredible power, spirits," he would say. Or "They are sacred, you know. We depend on them for everything. Never underestimate the love of a tree." And "Protect them from your people, especially the oil and lumber companies. And the cattle ranchers."

Then he announced that he would conduct healings on any people who felt the need. "This will involve a shapeshift," he said. "What I call a 'spirit shift,' because only the spirits see it. To the rest of you I will be just an old man sitting here on my stool. But the spirits will see me transform myself into a great fire-breathing volcano. The mountain will blow its top off. A raging river will burst forth and rush down the volcanic slopes into the person being healed. This river will form whirlpools and they will suck out the bad spirits that cause the illness. These spirits take the form of *tsentsak*, invisible darts—like our blowgun darts. You will see this old man here on this stool regurgitating those poisonous darts and you will know that the river has cleansed the patient."

Many people wanted healings. Kitiar asked each to lie down on a bench in front of the stool where he sat. He began by brushing them gently with branches, in rhythm to his chanting, and spraying them with alcohol. Then the brushings became more forceful, the chanting louder. It was dark in the lodge except for a slight glow from the embers of the fire. I sat next to him so that I could translate, occasionally assisting him in any way I could. As close as I was I could not see him. I could hear him and feel his presence, but I could not so much as discern his outline. In most cases he performed extractions by literally sucking on the part of the patient where the illness was most pronounced and then regurgitating. I sensed that many of the healings were very powerful, and this sense was verified by the reactions of the patients. Many became highly emotional. One woman who had suffered from migraines for many years told me that when Kitiar sucked on her head she felt an incredible release, "as though someone unscrewed the top of a jack-in-the-box and that horrible devil inside went flying out!"

After everyone who wanted healings was finished, I took my place on the wooden bench. Kitiar scanned my body. "I know what you want," he said, and laughed. "But remember, it is dangerous—if you believe in death, if you believe in danger!" Then he camayed a mist of alcohol across me and began working with the branches. His chanting took me away from myself. I began to see geometric images that twisted themselves into other images, patterns merged to form flowers and animals. I felt cold and had the sensation that I had been transported into a dank cave. Suddenly I heard a shrill scream, then a flutter of wings, and I felt a wind blow over me. I realized that my eyes were closed. Opening them, I saw a huge bat hovering above me, its eyes peering down at me, its flapping wings fanning me. I screamed. The bat flew off.

Then Kitiar was helping me sit up. "I'm just an old shaman," he said. "Yet I can tell you that you must not be afraid. If you want to shapeshift, you have to have courage. Ask yourself: What do I fear?"

"You said it was dangerous."

"*If* you believe in danger . . . you must drop that belief."

"There is no danger?"

"Depends on how you look at it, doesn't it? In any case, it is the biggest problem you gringos have. You're obsessed with avoiding risks. I see it every time you bring people here. They always ask about the dangers—snakes, alligators, spiders, jaguars. We Shuar welcome death as our birth into another world."

"I agree—in principle. It's the actuality of the thing I have difficulty with."

"What is it that you fear about the shapeshift?"

"That I won't be able to return," I blurted out.

"And what's wrong with that?" He took a drink of trago and handed me the bottle. "I'll show you," he continued. "It's my time, you know. I must leave all this work to you and others."

"What are you saying?" I felt anxious over all his talk of leaving. He had said he would become a bat. I had seen enough not to doubt him. So, what did he mean about leaving?

"You'll see. You've already seen it, in fact. My last lesson for you is one of courage. You must not have fear. Take risks."

Three months later I brought another group of North Americans into the rainforest. Kitiar had previously agreed to come to the lodge where we were spending our nights and conduct a special ceremony. Raul and I prepared the group. Everyone was very excited about this opportunity to work with one of the last of the great traditional Shuar shamans. I could barely contain myself—I had so much to share with Kitiar and so many questions I hoped he would answer. We built up the fire, set out candles and gifts that some of the people had brought. We waited.

"*Mañana*," someone quipped as we sat staring into the flames. "The word sort of takes on new meaning, doesn't it?"

"Perhaps this is what the shamans really mean when they talk about 'parallel worlds' and 'nonordinary reality,'" another joked.

The Shuar family we were living with chanted for us and showed us how to brew chicha, the beer made from the manioc (cassava) plant. A very important part of the Shuar diet and ritual, the plant is considered sacred; only women are allowed to produce the beer. They sat before a great earthen vat, dipping their fingers into the chopped roots that had been boiled to the consistency of mashed potatoes, chewing and spitting into the vat where the liquid would ferment overnight.

"For the Shuar," I explained, "chicha is the potato, bread, and rice—their main source of starch and carbohydrates."

This was followed by an exchange of one-liners. I was glad for the humor. Earlier I had told the group that, although shamans consider their work to be sacred, they never take themselves or their lives too seriously. The trickster side, the playful child, keeps the pensive adult in balance.

We waited patiently until late into the night. Our cook, Lucho, brought out a guitar and played for us. I had heard his music often enough before, but this time was different. He chose sad songs, songs of betrayal and death, melancholic music that weighted the air down with sadness.

Suddenly I heard a shrill whistle. I looked up in time to see a large bat dart through the door, over Lucho's head and into the rafters. I glanced around. Others in the group were pointing excitedly at it. By now everyone had seen it. The Shuar family flew into a panic. The children beat on kettles, the women shouted. The bat flew down, circled us once as if saluting us, and exited out the doorway through which it had entered.

The Shuar chattered among themselves. They appeared agitated. Our group wanted to know what they thought had caused the bat to fly in.

"Someone died," Tantar, the family head, told us. "His spirit passed into the bat. It came to say goodbye."

I had a sinking feeling in the pit of my stomach. But I said nothing.

Early the next morning while we were preparing breakfast, Kitiar's son, Kutsa, stumbled up to the lodge where we had waited all the night before for his father. Exhausted, he collapsed onto a stool. "Kitiar has gone," he said. The group gathered around him.

"Gone where?" Raul asked.

"Disappeared. Vanished." The Shuar family brought him a bowl of chicha, which he quickly drained. Then he told us an incredible story.

About a month earlier three Shuar shamans and a person Kutsa described as "a gringo missionary" accused Kitiar of practicing black magic— a terrible accusation in the Shuar culture. "I believe," Kutsa said, "that it was the Company. They hated him." During my translation, I explained that "the Company" was a term applied to foreign tree-cutting and oil interests; the indigenous community saw them all as one big adversary—or ally, depending on which side an individual took. According-ing to Kutsa, they launched a vicious campaign to discredit Kitiar. Fi-nally, the three shamans ordered him to appear before them so they could pass judgment on him. The rumor was that they intended to banish him from the community and burn his home.

Kutsa emphasized that Kitiar was not frightened personally—reminding me of the message the shaman had conveyed during my previous heal-ing—however, he was deeply concerned by the implications of these ac-tions. Kitiar told his son, "I am a man of integrity. My powers are for healing, not evil. There are people who want to destroy me because I fight the Company and protect the forests. They are evil. I must not give in to them. Time for me to move on."

Kutsa spent the night in his father's lodge. They worked together the next day preparing herbal remedies for an elderly woman who suffered from rheumatism. Late in the afternoon, Kitiar filled his gourd with chicha and swung his blowgun and a quiver of darts over his shoulder. He turned to his son. "Tell John I am sorry that he won't see Kitiar the shaman tonight. But he will see me." He walked away from his home. Kutsa heard him say, "Have courage."

"He just melted into the jungle." Kutsa looked up and around at the faces staring at him. He smiled. "Into his trees."

Chapter 12

Being the "Other"

Kitiar's disappearance disturbed me deeply. I thought about him frequently. One time he came to me in a dream and told me to be sure that the people who went on our trips took their responsibilities seriously. He reminded me that we had named our trips Dream Change Adventures: Serving Earth Through Self-awareness. "Be sure," he admonished, "that it isn't just the self-awareness part that brings the people. They must be committed to serving the earth, changing the dream to one that honors Nunqui, goddess of the plants, and Tsunqui, spirit of the waters."

After that I was careful to point out the destructive aspects of the trips whenever I spoke about them. During my lectures and workshops I would describe the fragility of rainforest ecology. "Every person who enters the rainforest hurts it," I would say. "We also bring confusion to the Shuar themselves. Our presence puts pressure on their family lives and, especially among the young people, may raise questions about the validity of their traditional ways." I discussed the negative influences of the missionaries, how they had taught the indigenous communities that a person can forget about the oral traditions once he or she learns to read, and that firsthand knowledge of plants can be ignored since books provide a long-term record.

But I always added that, by showing genuine respect for the knowledge of the elders and the healing abilities of the shamans, we reinforce their powers. "When the young Shuar see us sitting at the feet of the shamans, listening to their stories, and when our medical doctors come to learn from them about healing—that speaks very clearly."

I would end this discussion by summarizing my personal philosophy, one that reached back into my past as an economist. "It is a benefit–cost issue. If we return to the States determined to change the dream of our people, to cut back on materialism, including consumption of the oil, lumber, and beef that is laying waste to the rainforests, then the benefits will outweigh the costs of our visit."

I began to introduce the concept of shapeshifting into my workshops. I knew I could not teach participants to be a bush, the way Toyup had done it; I had not accomplished this myself. Besides, doing so required a philosophical adjustment that I doubted many were prepared to make, an acceptance that a bush is equal to a person, that a hierarchy among species does not exist and thus there is no need to fear not returning. However, I could at least encourage the participants to consider such possibilities; I could discuss the idea of physical, cellular transformation and the benefits of shapeshifting our perceptions, lifestyles, and institutions. In addition to talking, I initiated seven exercises—psychonavigational journeys—that helped bring shapeshifting into focus for many of the participants.

The first of these I learned while Raul and I accompanied a group through Ecuador. We had spent the night with a Quechua woman shaman, Iyarina, high in the Andes at an altitude of over ten thousand feet. Early in the morning, while it was still dark, she led us through the cold mountain air to the sacred spring of her people. As the day began to announce its arrival, opening like a brilliant orange and yellow blossom across the volcanic peaks, we watched the water gushing up out of Pachamama to form a splendid stream that would make its way down the slopes into the Amazon, and eventually all the way to the Atlantic Ocean.

"In a moment," Iyarina told us in her soft voice that, despite its gentleness, seemed to echo from the mountains, "we will greet Inti, the sun. This spring's name is Pocvio Juanita; her feminine spirit will join the masculine spirit of the sun. Feel them unite and shapeshift into you. Be aware of the strong male and female forces flowing together inside you, of the balancing that occurs between fire and water." She smiled. "Feel the earth beneath your feet and the air as Pachamama breathes on you, camaying over and through you. This is a shapeshift of the four elements. All join together within you." She turned and with her eyes took in each of us. "Within us. We are one."

We followed her as she turned from the spring toward the East and raised her arms in the direction of the sun. As if on cue, it popped over the top of a glacier-capped peak, like a ball that has been held under water and suddenly released, nearly blinding us.

She stepped forward, bending her front leg so that the knee of the back one nearly touched the ground. Simultaneously, she brought her hands in from the sun and down over her head and body, an elegant motion that appeared to draw the energy into her. Her voice resounded clearly in the thin Andean air, stretching out the Quechua name from the moment she began with her hands extended to the sun to when she ended, palms down, inches from the ground: "Iiiiinnnnnnn-ti." It was a dance and chant, unadorned yet powerful in its simplicity, which she invited us to join. We followed her, trying to maintain our balance as we moved across the rough earth. We repeated the invocation three times. Then, like her, we drew ourselves erect and turned slowly around, allowing the sun to bathe our backs.

She asked us to focus on the spring and repeated the process, this time bringing in the power of water. After that she continued with earth and air.

Despite the early hour, the high altitude, and the fact that we had been up late the night before, the experience left me—and I believe the others—feeling energized and balanced. I was very aware of the four elements; it was as though they had fused into a highly charged yet relaxing force inside me—a sensation that lasted all day.

Iyarina later explained that we could do this back in our homes. Even if you live in a city apartment, she said, you could use a bowl of water instead of the spring and face East even if you could not see the sun. "The air is always there around you and the earth is below, regardless of whether you are on the ground or on the tenth floor. Use the English names, if that is easier. It is the spirit and your intent that counts. You are air, water, earth, and fire, male and female. Be the power of all of them, the spirit that is balanced."

As I was teaching this at one of my workshops, I recalled the journey into the stone that Viejo Itza had taught me. This led to the second shapeshifting exercise. I encouraged participants to find a stone—or some other object that had touched the ground—during their lunch break. I told them about the technique Viejo Itza had showed me, how to psychonavigate into the stone and see inside it something that needed to change, either in their personal lives or in the larger community. I repeated my own teacher's words. "Go into the stone and feel it enter your heart. Shapeshifting is about energy, spirit. If you don't understand something, ask questions. Find out what needs to shift."

These stones, called *huacas,* which in Quechua means "sacred items," also became a psychonavigational tool, a type of spirit guide. Participants learned that they did not have to carry the huacas with them in the physical sense in order to utilize their powers. The huacas were internalized and as such could always be called on for help.

The third exercise was inspired by one in Paulo Coelho's *The Pilgrimage,* the story in which he shapeshifts into a dog in order to fight the devil. This one, however, is a journey into the plant spirit that is us. I often suggest to participants that many of us have been plants in past lives. This belief was held by Toyup and the exercise is similar to one he practiced. It is about being the plant within. It can be done anywhere—even indoors—yet it can be especially powerful when done outside, in a forest or a park.

"Start by kneeling, with your eyes closed," I tell them, "your knees and lower legs on the ground; your body pulled down into a ball, forehead against your knees; arms beside your legs; fingers closed into fists. Feel the energy of the seed, the desire to burst into the plant. Visualize that energy surrounding you like an aura. Remember that seeds have the power to send shoots through concrete. Look deep into yourself to see how you want to use this energy, this power, what aspects of yourself you most desire to emphasize, to mature into the full-grown plant, to send out as flowers. Slowly allow your fingers to open, your head to rise. Feel the plant beginning to come alive, sprouting from the seed. Let yourself move as your inclinations dictate, eventually standing and reaching out with your arms, all the while continuing to feel the spirit of the plant. With eyes still closed, see what is around you—other plants, perhaps animals.

Listen to the voices, experience the sensations of being a plant, gain the wisdom of this world. Reach up and pull into yourself all the aspects of being that you honor most and desire to experience, to have manifest."

I suggested that they utilize a fourth exercise to help them complete the work they had begun in the two previous ones. I described the Tibetan star technique Marina had taught me, outlining the eight steps and the importance of taking action every day as well as verbalizing the intent and the commitment. Together, journeys 2, 3, and 4 provided a system for identifying things that needed to be transformed and for initiating the transformation itself.

The fifth exercise was one aimed at helping people to release aspects of themselves they no longer need or desire. While the others had concentrated on the importance of "shifting into," this one was about "shifting out of." It was modeled after the traditional fire ceremony of the Maya who live in the highlands of Guatemala.

Each participant is instructed to make a doll out of branches, flowers, leaves, grasses, or other flammable materials from nature. The doll represents the person who makes it, although it does not have to take on the appearance of a human or a traditional doll. Permission is asked of the materials before they are incorporated into the doll. While assembling it, the maker blows the spirit of something to be released into it; in other words, the participant focuses on shifting some aspect of his or her life, personality, or attitude into the doll. This could relate to an emotion (such as fear), a love relationship, an addiction, a job, or a physical ailment—in short, anything with which we feel a sense of "dis-ease." Afterward, the participant spends time meditating with the doll, continuing to send the spirit or energy of the aspect to be released into it. Later we hold a fire ceremony that includes chanting and bathing ourselves with the elements, as in Iyarina's exercise. At the end each participant presents his or her doll to the fire, which consumes it in flames, taking away the dis-ease and recycling it through Pachamama. This exercise can also be done by individuals and small groups using candles or an alcohol fire in a metal pan.

As I conducted these workshops I was quite aware that I myself had never shapeshifted in the physical sense, on a cellular level. I felt that Viejo Itza and Kitiar had prepared me for it as best they could and that now it was up to me to make my own attempt. I had faith that it could be done, and I had no doubts about what I had seen. I understood the basic theory and also that it was not so much a matter of technique as attitude. The secret lay in the heart, not the brain. What was required was a perceptual leap, a very basic dream change. That, and breaking through a major barrier—I knew I had to release my fears.

The trips themselves would prove to be an ally, consistently validating the incredible powers of shapeshifting. Many of the people who journeyed with me to Ecuador had problems, dis-eases, that were healed. When pressed for explanations, the shamans would often emphasize that instead of making the dis-ease vanish, they preferred to shift its energy into a form that would benefit the patient. (They often used words such as *vibration* or *air* rather than *energy*.)

People were healed of cancers, migraines, serious back problems, chronic fatigue syndrome, colitis, knee and ankle injuries, infertility, eyesight failure, addictions to cigarettes, alcohol, food, and sex, and a host of emotional problems centered around relationships with parents, lovers, spouses, and children, as well as issues concerning self-worth, careers, and prosperity. Every one of these healings was witnessed by other group members, including medical doctors and psychiatrists. They have been documented in several television specials aired in the United States. One entitled *Shaman Healers*, produced by Paramount Pictures, features a woman who was diagnosed with an ovarian tumor before departing her home in Seattle, was healed by a Quechua shaman, and was pronounced "unexplainably cured" by her physician when she returned home.

Several people went through spectacular cellular changes after the shamanic healings. An example is a woman who had suffered chronic fatigue syndrome for ten years without receiving any relief from numerous medical doctors and other medical professionals. Immediately after her healing by a Shuar shaman, we on the trip noted a significant change in her appearance; she seemed much "lighter" in her energy—thinner and happier. She said she felt "a hundred times better, as though a great weight has been lifted." Several days later, she flew home. When she got off the plane, her husband and son were waiting for her at the gate. She walked up to them but they failed to recognize her. She stood directly in front of them; they continued to search for her among the exiting passengers until she spoke to them. Her profound healing led her to make several return trips to Ecuador, along with her husband and son.

Another example is that of Joyce, a psychotherapist who told me, "I came on this trip because of my interest in alternative therapies, but know very little about shamanism. However, I was told by a spiritual counselor that I would receive a transfer of energy from a shaman and that it will change my life." Suffering from a problem of being perpetually overweight and exhausted, Joyce had experimented with many different diets, but to no avail. When we visited a Quechua shaman in his Andean home, she said she knew he was the one who would change her life. She was the first in her group to receive a healing, during which the shaman camayed alcohol through a candle, engulfing her in a fireball.

The next morning when I arrived at breakfast, I found the group huddled around her. Not only did she look happier, but also lighter in an emotional sense. "Can you believe that!" a physician who had known Joyce for years exclaimed. "Look at how radiant she is. She looks like a new person! Wait until my associates hear about this!"

Despite a very apparent change in emotions and attitude, Joyce's body was still burdened with excessive weight. When we reached the rainforest a day later, it posed serious obstacles for her; the long and arduous hike to the thermal waterfalls is taxing even for athletes in training. Although optional, Joyce insisted on giving it a try. She was not conditioned for this type of activity, but her heroic determination and newfound sense of self provided the support she needed. These and the encouragement of her friends allowed her to persevere; she completed the trek.

Bathing in the steaming waters of the volcanic falls, Joyce turned to me. "I feel absolutely transformed," she beamed. Her next words shocked me. "Would you consider me as a candidate to lead future trips?"

A few months after returning to the States Joyce had lost sixty pounds without dieting or undertaking any conscious effort to do so. Her energy level increased exponentially. She has become a trip leader—an excellent one who inspires others with her tireless enthusiasm and who, within a year of her first visit to Ecuador, had co-led two groups with me and one of her own. At many of our workshops we show a one-hour television special about the original trip she was on; people in the audience who see her standing next to her image on the screen cannot believe it is the same person. One day about a year after that first trip she sent me the following message via e-mail:

> I forgot to tell you this about my cellular change. I began to get a rash on my back about two months after I returned from Ecuador. It was strange because it was underneath the skin. The rash never broke the skin, but my skin became red and itchy. No topical ointments did any good. Finally the doctor had blood work done and prescribed a medication that eventually did take care of the rash. What the blood work showed, as I recall it, was that my body was having a reaction at the level of the cells and the blood. There was inflammation of the blood cells. The cells were responding as if there was an infection but the M.D. was so perplexed because there was no infection. He called it a vascular reaction. He strongly felt that the cells were reacting to something but he had no clue what it was. I knew the rash was a reaction to the change going on in my body—there was never any doubt about that for me. The M.D. said he had never seen anything like it. He thought it all was very strange.

These experiences in Ecuador led me to begin practicing two more psychonavigation exercises. Each involves the snake, an animal whose power is recognized by nearly all shamanic cultures, yet whose image in our own culture often takes on frightening, even evil, connotations. I found these journeys so personally empowering that I introduced them into my workshops.

In the first of these (the sixth in the shapeshifting series), I ask people to journey to the snake. By this time they have a spirit guide, like the one camayed into me by Maria Quischpe, or a huaca, similar to Viejo Itza's stone. They are encouraged to take one or both with them. The only instructions are for them to get to know the snake, to experience it through as many senses as possible. Each person's journey is unique: some study the snake's appearance and habits; others watch its birth (from an egg or directly from its mother), follow its growth, and witness it shedding its skin; others may focus on its energy fields; some devote their time to understanding how their attitudes toward the snake evolved and how these impact their lives.

The next exercise may lead directly into a physical shapeshift. I tell participants to *be* the snake. We share stories about the anaconda, considered divine by many Amazon cultures. We discuss the snake symbolism of the Egyptian, Celtic, Tantric, and other traditions. I point out that initiates into shapeshifting often begin by being the snake and shedding their old skins. This technique has been practiced for as long as human history has been recorded. I encourage them to feel their own integration into this ancient heritage. It is a time for leaving behind fears, forgetting the hierarchal concepts schools have drummed into us. The snake is a primal teacher, so powerful that every major, nonecstatic religion has felt threatened by it. I suggest that this journey offers the opportunity to escape all those debilitating prejudices. "Let the snake take over! Open up to its mystery! Crawl on the floor, coil, hissss . . ."

I have been told by countless workshop participants that these seven journeys provide an inspirational and enlightening introduction to shapeshifting. The last two that emphasize the potency of the snake provide a format for entering into the cellular shapeshift. One woman who said she had always been terrified of serpents confessed, "Now I understand why the snake has assumed such an important role in our psyches since the time of the earliest cave drawings. I am eternally indebted to the snake that is me."

A man summarized his feelings by asking, "Should any historian be surprised to learn that the snake was the symbol of the Celtic shamans—the Druids—and that Bishop Patrick (later Saint Patrick) had to drive them out before he could secure the authority of the Catholic Church in Ireland?"

Winifred had recently inherited an old wing-backed chair from her grandmother, the type that has a large semicircle above each of the overstuffed arms looking something like a shield. I have been told they were so designed to protect a person seated in the chair from winter drafts. The chair was solid white and extremely comfortable. I was very fond of the chair and sat in it every evening when I was home. One night Winifred, exhausted from a business trip, went to bed early. I sat in the chair sipping a beer and listening to a tape I had made of Kitiar chanting. An odd feeling came over me that I and the chair had been connected in some previous life; that the chair had been my ally, and had protected me.

At least twice a day after that I sat in the chair and meditated. I tried to release every thought and feeling except those that seemed centered around the chair. I also practiced the dream-change technique of determining whether my desire to shapeshift into the chair was a dream or fantasy. The answer was unambiguous—it was a dream. This led to the next step. I practiced the Tibetan star technique Marina had taught me, sending my dream of being the chair into the star and bringing them both inside my head and heart.

I had been doing these practices for nearly two months when Jessica challenged me to a game of hide-and-seek. We decided to add an element of drama to it by arming ourselves with toy dart guns my father had given us for Christmas as a gag gift. I was losing badly and, a half hour or so into the game, had begun to feel not only humiliated but also a bit desperate to win one. Jessica disappeared into her bedroom to count. I raced into the living room and in a panic cast about for a hiding place. There was that chair. I was drawn to it. I felt a certainty that I could do it. Looking down at my clothes, I recalled Toyup's observation about colors: I was wearing khaki shorts and a red T-shirt. I dashed into my closet and grabbed my white terry cloth bathrobe. I left my dart gun on a closet shelf. I slipped into the chair, pulling the bathrobe over me, and focused on feeling my energy merge with that of the chair, another aspect of my being. I quickly journeyed to the snake and, by discarding its skin, released my fears.

Pretty soon I heard Jessica's footsteps. She was approaching from the kitchen, cautiously. I saw her enter the living room. I shut my eyes and let myself be the chair. Like a distant echo, I heard her walking toward me. I held my breath. I heard her breathing, as though she were right in front of me. I knew she was there, not more than a couple of feet away, probably staring at me the chair.

Then she left. I knew she was gone and, opening my eyes, spotted her as she sneaked into the hall toward our bedroom. I had a strong desire to be her father and laugh with her.

It could not have been more than a minute or two later when she returned. She jumped when she saw me, charged, and shot me with a dart. "Got you," she yelled victoriously. Then she tilted her head. "Why are you just sitting there? Where were you a moment ago?"

"I was right here in this chair."

"No way!" She reloaded her gun and aimed it at my feet. "Tell me the truth."

"I swear it—right here in this chair."

"Liar! I stood here right where I am now and looked under it and behind it. You weren't anywhere around."

"Not around. I was here. I was the chair."

"You think I'll fall for that? I suppose that stupid bathrobe camou-flaged you? If so, how come I found you just now?"

I explained to her what had happened. The concept of shapeshifting was, of course, not a new one to Jessica. Her mouth fell open. She stared at me. "Are you serious? You are, aren't you?"

That experience was a shock to all of us. I tried to repeat it for Winifred, but I felt self-conscious and apprehensive. It did not work. Like so many things we cannot explain, it slipped away, out of conversation and al-most out of mind. Yet it had definitely opened a door.

Not long after the hide-and-seek adventure, the three of us traveled together in Ecuador with Raul, his wife, Elsa, and their daughter, Lourdes. On the next to the last day Winifred had a healing by a Quechua shaman, Manco, who had been one of my first teachers. Following the healing Manco suggested that we go to the market on our way to the airport the next morning and purchase some herbs for Winifred to take home so she could prepare a tea that Manco assured us would help with her healings. He wrote a long list and instructed us to give it to a particular woman in the market, a renowned herbalist.

We were amazed by the volume of herbs the woman assembled for us and wrapped in a newspaper. The bundle was the size of one containing three or four dozen long-stem roses.

"How will we get it past airport security?" Winifred asked as we drove away. "These are live plants." At that time Ecuador was participating in a custom's program whereby United States–trained security guards searched all carry-on luggage at the boarding gate in Quito; checked bags were sent through sophisticated machines. Prohibitions against bring-ing live plants into the United States were strictly enforced. There were a couple of advantages to this system. First, it saved time in Miami. Second, if the plants were legal by Ecuadorian law and there had been no attempt to conceal them, they were merely confiscated; no laws had been broken, as would have been the case if the passenger had actually brought them into the US.

In order to avoid the possibility of criminal charges, we decided not to try to hide the herbs, but rather to simply leave them in Winifred's carry-on, completely obvious to anyone who cared to look. As we prepared to go through security Jessica reached inside, touched the bundle, and said "Be a newspaper."

Two uniformed soldiers stood behind a long table blocking the entrance to the American Airlines gate, meticulously searching every piece of carry-on luggage.

Jessica proceeded first. One of the soldiers pulled out her camera and motioned for her to open it. Fortunately she had removed her last roll of film before sending it through the X-ray machine. He peered inside and clicked the shutter several times, then returned it to her, nodding solemnly. Meanwhile, the other was rifling through the rest of the things in her bag: a sweater, four small Otavalan tapestries she had purchased for friends, a hairbrush, book, journal, pen, calculator, wallet, and cosmetics bag. These latter two stopped him. He demanded that she open first one and then the other. He examined every photo in her wallet and made her unscrew the top of each jar of cream and lipstick. When she lifted the top of her compact, he tapped the pad with his fingers, raising little puffs of talcum powder. He inserted a fingernail behind the mirror to see if he could pry it loose.

This was no trivial matter, no ordinary search. These men either had been warned that someone was trying to escape Ecuador with something very important or they were determined to impress an invisible superior. I had never experienced anything like it before.

Jessica was motioned on, into the gate area.

I nudged Winifred forward. I certainly did not want to go ahead and leave her there alone. As I watched her step up to the table, a feeling of panic grabbed me. I had no doubt that the soldiers would confiscate her bundle of herbs. And I had suddenly lost all confidence about the legality of what we were doing. How, I wondered, would they react to that assortment of shamanic "drugs"?

The first thrust his hands deep inside her duffel bag. He pulled out a light blue sweater, patted it down and, satisfied, tossed it to her. Then he began to lay other objects on the table. They came slowly—for me, painfully so—an apparent imitation of the items Jessica carried: a book, purse, cosmetics bag, brush, pencils, calculator. He pried the bag open wider and peered in. Then a wicked smile crossed his face, the first expression of emotion I had witnessed on either soldier. He reached in. I held my breath and glanced at Jessica who stood poised at the gate entrance looking back at us, tension etched into every line of her body. The soldier muttered to his companion and then pulled something out—a copy of *Cosmopolitan*! The two of them gawked at the scantily clad model on the cover. Then the soldier casually began tossing the things he had laid out on the table back into the bag. He handed it to Winifred and waved her forward. She was cleared. We were safe.

My head was spinning as I went through the formalities of the search. I kept thinking about that bundle of herbs. Where had it gone?

Finally the security search was over. I passed through the gate to find Jessica and Winifred seated inside, barely able to control the relief they felt. "Right here," Winifred said, pointing at her bag in answer to my question. "In plain sight all the time. The biggest thing inside. I don't know how they missed it. It was as though it simply disappeared."

"Shapeshifted into a newspaper," Jessica corrected.

Several months later I found myself in that same Quito airport exiting the country with sixteen people who had just spent ten days with me and the shamans. Several of them carried spears they had purchased from the Shuar.

Since the Shuar fashion their spears from extremely hard chonta wood, they do not attach stone or metal tips to them. Instead, they carve a triangular spearhead out of the dark wood, a spearhead strong enough to pierce the toughest hide of an animal—or an enemy. The shape of the triangle and the length of the shaft tell a great deal about the intended use of the spear. Long, narrow heads are designed for fishing. Thicker ones are for hunting animals. Spears with smaller heads and serpents crafted into their shafts are ceremonial. Combat spears—those used to take another man's life—have diamond-shaped heads that taper off to brutal points.

This day I, too, carried a spear. It had been made for me as a special gift from one of the shamans, for the express purpose of "wiping out the evil warriors who destroy the forests." Although this intent was clearly symbolic, a reference to the spirit of those people who manage oil companies and other non-earth–honoring organizations—not for killing them physically—it was, nonetheless, a true combat weapon. About five feet tall, like all war spears it was sturdy and simple, made for thrusting, not throwing. It was adorned with blood-red toucan feathers and its diamond head was sharpened to a lethal point. There could be no doubt that I carried a weapon—one that had no place inside the cabin of the American Airlines Boeing 757 we were about to board.

The night before, several of the group members had made bets about whether they could get away with carrying their spears onto the plane. They took great pains to disguise them. One man plastered the head of his with wads of wet paper which he then covered with a red bandanna to make it look, he said, "like a walking stick." A woman fastened a woven tapestry to hers and then rolled it onto the shaft in a way that gave it the appearance of a furled flag. Someone found a section of rubber hosing on a trash pile outside the hacienda where we spent that last night and managed to stuff his long, slim fishing spear inside.

In the bus on the way to the airport, I took the microphone. Holding my spear high, I announced that I would shapeshift it into a cane and take it aboard the plane. I don't know what possessed me to do this, perhaps a memory of that other success with Winifred's herbs; yet, I felt an overwhelming confidence that I could do it. My announcement brought peals of laughter. In answer to several questions, I stated publicly that this was no joke, that I would do absolutely nothing to disguise or hide the spear. "A true test for the shapeshifter," I bragged, with perhaps a bit too much bravado.

Now, once again at the Quito airport, I faced those same two soldiers stationed behind their table, or two who appeared identical. As is my custom, I allowed all the group to precede me. One by one the spears were confiscated, their owners given baggage claims and assurances that they could pick them up in Miami.

I stepped to the table. The soldiers pawed through my backpack, making a complete mess of its contents. Then they let me pass. My fellow travelers looked on in amazement as I entered the gate area, spear in hand.

"The flight attendants will get you," the woman whose "flag" had been seized sneered.

I was not at all surprised myself when, thirty minutes later, I breezed past the woman checking boarding passses and the size of carry-ons at the door of the plane and then three other flight attendants without a problem. One looked directly at my spear. Then she raised her eyes to mine and gave me a big grin. "Did you climb Mt. Chimborazo?" she asked.

I nodded sheepishly and hurried down the aisle.

A master teacher for decades to some of the best Quechua shamans, Manco had always declined my invitations to come to the United States, saying that he had no desire to abandon the spirits of the high Andes. I had studied under Manco for many years; recently he had begun to teach Jessica. Working with her had a strong influence on him. It apparently changed his mind about coming to the States. At first he talked about the importance of bringing the earth-honoring philosophy of shamanism to the young people of North America; he charged me with this responsibility. Then he started thinking about the powerful bridge that could be built through South-North interchanges. He related to Jessica the ancient legends about the Condor and the Eagle mating during the Fifth Pachacuti.

One day as we sat beneath the snowcapped peak of Cotopaxi, the world's highest active volcano, he turned to me with a smile. "Experience is everything," he said. "I need to experience the land of the Eagle."

Jessica made extensive preparations for his visit. She placed huacas, flowers, and potted plants around the room that would be his, and hung Quechua tapestries to make him feel at home. Winifred pointed out that our house was already adorned with ample mementos from the Andes and Amazon—Quechua rugs and pottery, silver and gold images of Mama Kilya and Inti, Shuar dance belts, necklaces, and spears, Achuar blowguns—as well as an assortment of art from various shamanic cultures around the world. But this did not inhibit Jessica in the least. "His room needs to be special," she said. She even brewed a tea for him from the leaves of the ancient oak tree that stands beside our house. This surprised me because, although I often work with that tree to receive energy and healing power, I had never before seen it infused into a tea. When I asked where she had learned this, she told me that it had been a "hunch."

It was his first visit to the United States, but all the asphalt, traffic, pollution, and loud confusion of Miami did not seem to phase Manco. He walked up to a skyscraper, touched it gently, and proclaimed, "A beautiful spirit, very feminine, like Cotopaxi." He took it all in and brought the sense of oneness with him. We were delighted to see that his ecstasy was not dependent upon being in Ecuador.

Manco's first full day at our house was devoted to healings. I had let a few close friends know that he would be coming. The word spread quickly. He did twenty-seven healings that day, using the techniques he knew so well. For a number of people he prescribed herbal teas and baths as follow-up, as he had done that time in the Andes for Winifred. When the healings were finished, I pointed out to him that many of those plants were indigenous to the Andes and not readily available in tropical Florida. He suggested we suspend the healings for a day.

Early in the morning, before Jessica left for school, he led her on a little tour of our yard. Winifred, Jessica, and I are plant lovers. In addition to those plants common to most Florida yards, such as oranges, grapefruits, ficus, bougainvillea, mango, and avocado, we have many that are considered by our neighbors to be rather exotic. These plants include datura, ayahuasca, passionflower, frangipani, mahogany, gardenia, San Pedro, date palm, and a rare gyger tree.

Manco discovered varieties I had never noticed. Unlike most Floridians, we use no fertilizers, insecticides, or water (other than rain). When we bought our house we also ended up owning a sophisticated underground sprinkler system. We never turn it on. Consequently, the golf course grass died out and was replaced with a native variety, what the neighbors refer to as grab grass. Among the leaves of this "inferior" variety, Manco found some wondrous healing plants that he was familiar with. However, he had never before seen most of the plants that he encountered that morning.

"Now," he told Jessica, "You will learn how to talk with the plants when you don't already know them. The first step: You must be them."

Manco spent the rest of the day psychonavigating into the different plants. After Jessica went off to school, I joined him. I asked whether he and she had learned anything important.

"A lot," he assured me. He proceeded to tell me that the live-oak tea Jessica had brewed should not really be used as a tea at all, but rather, that it would make a good salve to use against skin rashes, especially those generated by other plants. "Jessica and I found that out together."

I asked how they had accomplished this.

"Just sit here in front of this little flower," he told me, pointing at a heavenly blue morning glory. "Let your spirit join its spirit. Merge your energy fields."

"Isn't that a form of shapeshifting?"

He admitted that it was, adding, "If we can let go of the human armor we wear. All you have to do is journey into a plant, be it, and learn its secrets."

I tried to follow his example, but I had difficulty doing it. My mind got in the way. I knew that this little flower contained ingredients similar to those used to synthesize LSD—that powerful hallucinogenic that had been so popular during my college years. This bit of book knowledge seemed to deter me from taking the journey he apparently was on. My curiosity was aroused. I found myself continually wondering what he would discover about this plant.

"Wow!" he exclaimed at last. "Very powerful for such a tiny flower. A plant for dreaming." He caressed it lovingly. "I'm not sure how to use you yet." He looked at me. "A wonderful plant, one that deserves respect. I need more time with this one before prescribing it to anyone."

After lunch I had to return to my office to make phone calls and deal with several business issues. Manco continued his work with the plants. In mid-afternoon I decided to take a break.

I walked around the house looking for him, but he was not to be found. I went inside, shouted for him, checked the bathroom, and then took another turn around the house, completely covering our modest property for the second time. No Manco. Assuming that he had decided to stroll down the street, I returned to my office and continued to work.

But something bothered me. We live on a small residential street. Manco's walking options were limited. I decided I had better go looking for him. I started out our driveway. A movement caught my eye. Off to my left, I spied him. He seemed to be stepping out from behind the tall date palm that guards a corner of our property. I rushed up to him, relieved to have found him there, and asked where he had been.

"Right here," he grinned.

"Impossible!" I had actually circled that tree twice in the last fifteen minutes.

"Right here," he insisted. "This tree the whole time."

I could not hold back the laughter. "You dropped your armor."

He slapped his knees and broke into a fit of childlike giggling. At last he regained control and, wiping the tears from his eyes, peered into mine. "I dropped my armor."

That evening over dinner, Winifred listened to Jessica's stories about plants and to Manco's revelations that he had discovered six new teas and five baths. Then she confessed she had a story of her own. She explained that an engineer she worked with had invested money in a small firm in England that developed organic medicines. "He received a fax today with good news. The company is marketing a new organic salve that has proven effective against poison ivy." She turned in her chair toward the window. "Its main ingredient is the bark of that tree out there— the live oak."

Chapter 13

Shapeshifting a Deadly Virus

Before disappearing, the shaman Kitiar had commanded us to shift our people. He had said that we should bring more of them to learn from the Shuar and then help them go out and teach others in the North. He had also predicted his departure from this world, although at the time none of us had been astute enough to understand the full implications of what he had said. But he had departed exactly as he had predicted; he had transformed himself into a bat and flown away.

Now that Kitiar was gone, Raul and I felt a deep obligation to honor his wishes. He had been a great teacher, a master for both of us. He had been like a father and brother. We not only believed that we owed it to him to carry out his last instructions, we also knew that he understood things beyond our comprehension. Who were we to question his insights? And there was something else that motivated us; I am certain Raul felt it as strongly as I, although we never discussed it. We feared that by not complying we might incur his wrath. It was not a rational view, yet the things we had experienced left no doubt in our minds about his powers as a shaman and shapeshifter.

During a period of three years we took sixteen different groups into the Andes and Amazon, a total of 230 people. These were profound experiences, not only for the people we led but also for us. (Descriptions of many of these experiences can be found in my book *The World Is As You*

Dream It.) In addition, during this time I personally worked with shamans in the Andes and Amazon. I felt that shapeshifting was becoming
part of my life. Sometimes I wondered whether I had gone too far. There
were many occasions when I feared that I might be losing my sanity and
the ability to discern between the different levels of reality.

In 1994, Sarah, a dear friend and the wife of my college roommate,
was suddenly stricken by a mysterious and deadly virus. It took her, and
all of us, totally by surprise. William, her husband, was sitting at his desk
in his Palm Beach law office one afternoon when he received a phone call
from a heart specialist he had never met. The cardiologist informed him
that Sarah had been rushed to the hospital by her family doctor who had
been giving her a routine physical exam. At the emergency room they
had discovered that an infectious fluid filled her chest cavity. The radiologist could not even see her heart and lungs on the X ray.

Sarah was subjected to a series of intensive and often grueling exami-
nations. Tests showed that the fluid was caused by a rare virus for which
there was no known cure. The medical establishment threw up its hands
and, after ten days, sent Sarah home with virtually no hope of recover-
ing. Medical science offered no remedy. Just before Thanksgiving the
doctors warned William that he and their ten-year-old daughter, Jessica's
best friend, would probably be alone by Christmas.

Sarah, a thirty-six-year-old executive in an engineering company, had
never shared her husband's interest in shamanism. I have generally found
women to be more enthusiastic than men (60–70 percent of my workshop and trip participants are women). But William had been the family
member who joined one of my groups and journeyed to Ecuador while
Sarah stayed home with her career and daughter. Now she wondered
aloud whether the virus had been carried back by William. The doctors
assured them that this was highly unlikely; they explained that adults
almost never carry such viruses without it showing up in them and, besides, nearly a year had elapsed between his return and her illness. There
was simply no explanation for the disease.

One night while Winifred and Jessica slept, I went outside. The air
was clear, the stars brilliant. Moisture from a shower earlier in the evening
clung to the air and the smell of damp foliage reminded me of the Amazon. I thought about that night with Kitiar. I could almost see him sitting

on his stool beside the fire, encouraging me to have faith and courage. I wished he were with me now. As I gazed upward, I was drawn to one star. It seemed larger than all the others. Staring into it, I was amazed to see it turn to a bluish hue. Suddenly it seemed to blink. At first I thought it must be I who had blinked. Until it happened again. I squinted, changing my perspective. Now I saw that the star had not blinked at all, but that some object had moved across it, shadowing it. I focused on the movement. It came again. The star was blanketed for an instant, as though by wings. I was incredulous. It was a bat! The first I had seen at our house since moving in three years earlier.

I could barely believe my eyes, yet there it was. As my eyes adjusted, I watched it swooping and circling around an old tree in our backyard. I was deeply moved, astounded, and a bit frightened. I brought my hands up to my heart and bowed to the bat. I did this without thinking. "Kitiar," I said.

The next morning Sarah called and asked if I would come by her house to talk with her. When I arrived, she was propped up in her bed. She was pale and appeared fragile, almost childlike; an aura of peacefulness seemed to radiate from her. Seeing her this way reminded me of discussions with Viejo Itza about energy bodies and auras. As I sat next to her, sipping a cup of coffee William had prepared, she asked whether I could use shamanism to help her. Her request took me completely by surprise; of course, I could not refuse to try. I agreed to do a healing, combining techniques I had learned from Kitiar and other Shuar with those of Quechua shamans from the high Andes.

Over the years all my teachers have emphasized that we humans are not the healers. Each of them has told me, in his or her own words: "All healing comes from Pachamama, Mother Earth, Mother Universe. I am simply a conduit. Every human being has this ability, if we tap into Pachamama's dream. Be open to the patient's true desires; let the universe do the rest." I have heard this from shamans in Indonesia, Egypt, Iran, Italy, Thailand, Mexico, Panama, Brazil, Guatemala, Peru, Bolivia, Ecuador, and North America—the same message delivered in different languages and through a variety of rituals. "The specifics of the ceremonies, the techniques," I have been told time and time again, "are not important so long as they connect the patient with the powers of nature."

As Sarah lay in her bed, I asked her what she wanted.

"To live," she said. "To have more time with my family and this beautiful world."

I suggested, in as polite and delicate a manner as I could, that perhaps it was her time to move on. She smiled softly but spoke firmly. "I don't believe that. I know I have things left to do."

It was what I needed to hear. I instructed her to lie flat on her back and relax her whole body, to feel it sinking into the earth the way Viejo Itza had shown me. I walked outside and clipped small branches from three trees: mahogany, live oak, and brugmansia.

Back inside, I lit a candle next to her bed, placed a bowl of water and the small stone Viejo Itza had given me beside it, and fanned the leaves over her body, bringing each of the four elements close to her. I moved the branches in rhythm to Kitiar's chanting, which I could hear as clearly as if he had been seated next to me. I felt a deep compassion for Sarah and love for her husband and daughter. I called on Kitiar, Viejo Itza, and several other shamans to assist me. I asked Pachamama to do whatever was appropriate for Sarah. I felt a merging between us.

I released all thoughts and emotions, opening myself to whatever might come.

A tiny ball appeared. The size of a marble, it materialized like a sort of hologram of light near her heart. The thought intruded that it was just my imagination. Quickly I chased this thought away and returned to being the observer. The ball grew larger, to the size of a Ping-Pong ball; it had a bluish hue. It was not like a solid object; it appeared more fluid, and seemed to vibrate. It moved slowly around her chest cavity. I had the feeling that it was searching for something. I also had the feeling that I should try to enter it; however, something told me to be wary and to resist this temptation. I shook the branches more forcefully over her body. As I did so, the ball's color changed to a deeper blue, a color approaching black, then it sprouted two branches of its own, which it waved in unison with the rhythm of mine.

Its branches spread and flattened until they became wings. The ball had shifted itself into the shape of a bat. The movement of its wings imitated those of the bat that had covered the star. It darted about, then swooped through her torso, and I understood that it was drinking up the fluid that threatened her life. Again, this came to me in the form of a knowing, like intuition, or a thought that we are sure is correct yet do not understand how we know it. Then the bat lifted up out of her body, flew directly past me and to the open window behind me. Perched on the windowsill facing outside, it made spastic, jerking motions. I realized with a start that it was regurgitating the fluid it had extracted from Sarah.

The bat repeated this process half a dozen times. At one point I began to feel foolish. I suspected that I was imagining—or fantasizing—the whole thing. I wondered what Sarah was thinking. Then I told myself that I must not allow this to happen, I must not lose faith—to do so would destroy the possibility of a healing. But I could not help it—my rational self jumped in. I stood up and looked closely at Sarah. Her eyes were closed. She appeared to be sleeping. I sat back down and was shocked to discover that my shifting attitude, even my actions, had not impeded the bat in the least. The healing continued. I was amazed by this revelation, and extremely relieved.

Then, without any warning, the bat returned to its form as a ball. It grew lighter in color and smaller in size until it disappeared.

"Wow!" Sarah exclaimed. She sat up and beamed at me. "I feel lighter! What did you do?"

"Nothing," I admitted. I told her about the ball of energy that became a bat. I gave her as much detail as I could recall, including the story about Kitiar and the bat. "I did nothing, except watch." I ended by confessing that I thought I might be verging on insanity.

"I would have agreed a month ago," she said. "But I *know* I am better."

The next day the radiologist confirmed it. A measurable portion of the fluid had disappeared. He was totally surprised. He and the cardiologist shrugged their shoulders. "Sometimes these things happen," the cardiologist told William. "The body amazes us with its abilities to fight off infections. Let's see how she looks in a week."

We repeated the process three more times, leaving a day of rest between each session. Each was a replica of that first healing. Although Sarah was not scheduled for another x-ray until the following week, she was certain that her healing was complete. William was much more skeptical, probably because he did not dare raise his hopes too high.

The sun was shining brightly on judgment day. I joined the two of them for a mid-morning coffee, then William drove Sarah to the hospital.

The results were astounding. The fluid had completely disappeared. The doctors were flabbergasted. Within two weeks Sarah had recovered. The doctors were so confused and unsure of themselves that they recommended she travel from Palm Beach, Florida to Rochester, Minnesota so the famed Mayo Clinic could examine her.

Five days prior to Christmas, the Mayo Clinic reviewed the records of Sarah's old X rays and other tests, conducted a series of their own, and agreed that an unexplainable healing had occurred—a "miracle." The fact that it happened is recorded in the official books of Palm Beach Gardens Hospital and the Mayo Clinic.

About a month after Christmas, my friend and publisher Ehud Sperling called me. He and I had traveled together into Shuar territory shortly after his company published my first book, *The Stress-Free Habit*. He wanted to know if we could go again. "This time," he said, "Let's visit that old headhunter you told me about."

"The one who's killed more enemies than any other living Shuar?"

"Exactly. Thirty-three, I think you said."

"Tampur. Yes, that's what they tell me. I've never met him myself."

"Time you did." There was a pause. "And how about the Achuar? Can we get out to them?"

"I'm sure we can. Jaime is there. But it would be difficult. And dangerous."

"How dangerous?"

I summarized for him the story of Kitiar's disappearance. "Now you want to meet the most famous—infamous—of all the headhunters?" I reminded him that the Achuar are the archenemies of the Shuar, despite all their similarities and shared traditions. "You want to go visit a man who's killed more Achuar than any other living human, spend a few nights with him, and then move on across the territorial borders into the lands of his sworn enemies?"

"I thought the headhunting wars were over."

"Not entirely." I told him that just three months earlier two headless Shuar corpses had been discovered along a jungle trail. The incident had reopened the wounds of an ancient blood feud between two clans—one Shuar, the other Achuar.

"But isn't Tampur too old to get involved?"

"They say he's close to ninety. And that his powers as a wizard are phenomenal!"

"Black magic?"

"That's what I've heard. . . ."

"How can a writer like you pass up this opportunity? If you don't meet him now, you may never have another chance!"

My friend—or perhaps it was more in the role of my publisher—had embarrassed me into it. The next morning I got on the phone to Ecuador; within a week it had been arranged. Raul, Ehud, and I would fly deep into the jungle to visit Tampur. A young Shuar woman, Tayu, would travel with us, acting as guide, translator, and—most importantly—a sort of passport. The underlying and unspoken premise was that we would need a Shuar companion, and a woman would not be as likely to incite hostility as a Shuar man. I knew Tayu well; she was a beautiful young woman who had been trained as an herbal healer by her mother and had also attended the Catholic University in Quito. I was pleased by the choice and gratified that she had agreed to accompany us. Raul informed me that she was extremely excited by this opportunity to visit Tampur, a "grandfather" who she had not seen in many years. Desiring to record his stories and songs, she requested that we bring a tape recorder.

"I'm way ahead of you," Ehud said, when I called him with the news. "I bought a digital recorder just for this trip. Incredibly compact and high fidelity. A beautiful female Shuar healer and Tampur . . . should be quite an adventure!"

Chapter 14

Globes of Energy

Our single-engine Cessna had flown for about an hour in a light drizzle over unbroken rainforest. I sat up front next to the pilot, and Ehud and Tayu were behind me. Raul was wedged into the last seat, among our backpacks and sleeping bags.

Clouds swirled about, sometimes completely enveloping us. When I was able to look through them, I saw something below that struck me as different from other places in this same region. Perhaps, I told myself, it was just my imagination. Maybe it was because of the reputation of the man we were on our way to meet, or the knowledge that this was a land seldom reached by outsiders, that we had entered the very soul of the primeval forest. It is difficult to identify the origin of such perceptions, but from my vantage point, looking down, the top of the canopy appeared ethereal, misty, more like smoke than leaves. It seemed unreal, as if it were vibrating. Certain trees stood out above the others, like ancient sorcerers with tangled hair that faded in and out of focus, their long wizened arms reaching up to grasp our frail plane.

Yet I did not feel threatened. The feeling I had was more one of being beckoned, or seduced, like Odysseus with the Sirens. I had the urge to jump out of the plane. The thought struck me as funny: should I tether myself to the seat? Then I realized that I had already done that with the seatbelt.

I turned several times to see that Tayu and Ehud were engaged in conversation. Although she claimed not to speak English, she understood it well.

We passed from clouds to sunshine. The next thing I knew, we had landed on the airstrip in the Shuar community of Tampur.

Climbing out of the plane I felt the sun's heat. It almost knocked me over. I glanced around the clearing. The trees along its edges were immense, taller than any I had seen before. Like ancient gargoyles protecting a wizard's grotto, they cast giant shadows across the muddy runway.

Tayu led us to a lean-to beside the airstrip. Three Shuar women entered carrying gourds of chicha. Before I realized what had happened, I had accepted a bowl and found myself obliged to drink.

The three women were determined to demonstrate the popularity of their product. Each kept up a steady pace of forcing more and more upon us. Knowing that they were Tampur's daughters or daughters-in-law, none of us was about to refuse. All of it seemed unusually strong. When I lowered a bowl and gave it back, I was looking into the forest. I saw a movement, a mere shadow, along the still wall of vegetation. It might have been the chicha speaking to me, but I noticed that Tayu saw it too.

"Tampur," she said in a hushed voice. She rose and walked toward the shadow that materialized into a man. Tampur was reputed to have lived nearly a century; I had expected a shriveled, decrepit figure instead of the one that approached. The short, squat, potbellied Amazon native resembled Buddha more than a scarred old warrior.

Tampur was delighted to see Tayu. He greeted her like his own daughter. He expressed delight that we had come all this way to spend a night listening to his stories. He invited us to his lodge, about a half hour from the airstrip. If his physique had not impressed me, other qualities certainly did. Walking through the jungle, he reminded me of a jaguar. Not a muscle moved unless it was needed. He seemed aware of everything without paying attention to anything in particular. His eyes were those of a man who evaluates all that he sees and understands it in a glance. As old as he was there was no doubt in my mind that, in a fight, I would want him on my side.

That night we sat around the fire in Tampur's lodge. Ehud had brought his digital tape recorder and Tampur gave him permission to record his stories, saying that they were an important part of Shuar history that would vanish with him if someone did not make a record of them. With the help of one of the old warrior's great-grandsons, Ehud pounded a stake into the ground in front of Tampur and hung the microphone from it. Eyeing it suspiciously, Tampur lifted his machete as if about to strike, then laughed heartily.

As Tampur spoke clearly into the microphone, Tayu translated into Spanish and Raul or I tried to summarize in English for Ehud and the tape. Tampur admitted that he did not know his age; however, based on his experiences, Tayu estimated that he was between eighty and ninety years old. He told us about the internal wars that pitted Shuar family against Shuar family and about the great wars when the Shuar would unite to fight their common enemy, the Achuar. He personally had killed over thirty warriors. I asked to what he attributed his exceptional prowess.

"Certainly not my strength!" Laughing, he stood up and turned slowly around. "Always there were many who were much prettier and stronger. What I had was faith."

Tampur's wife handed me the chicha gourd. "That you would win?" I sipped the rich, cool drink.

"No. That I was doing what I was born to do." His eyes moved from one to another of us, lingering for a brief moment on each. "Losing is just as good as winning. The only important question is: Am I progressing down the path I was intended for? I am alive today not because I want to live more or am better with the spear than those who died before me, but because it is my destiny to be here talking to you, into this tiny little machine." He picked up his machete and, before any of us could react, tapped it against the microphone. Ehud, who was monitoring with earphones, jumped. Tampur broke into a fit of laughter.

I thought about what he had said. We in northern cultures are obsessed with the idea of succeeding or winning. Yet the great poets and philosophers of all times have pointed out that failure is an important part of life, that welcoming and honoring the declining, the aging, the dying side of us is essential if we are to live fully. I watched Tampur take the chicha gourd and reverently lift it to his lips. I recalled the Celtic poet David Whyte, who writes about the waning moon and the three days

*Ampan, Shuar warrior and traveling
companion to the author, with blowgun,
quiver of poison darts, and chicha pot.*
PHOTOGRAPH COURTESY OF VIVIAN DEITZ.

when the moon is in hiding. He likes to point out that people who are reluctant to face their "dark" sides, their failures, fears, and shortcomings, might just as well refuse to attempt to accomplish anything when the moon is in these phases.

"Have faith in your destiny," Tampur continued, handing the gourd to his wife. He stood to push a log into the fire. "Do as your spirit, your heart, directs. Don't think too much, the way my grandchildren are taught to do in the mission schools. Thinking is fine when we have to figure something out, like how to place a pole to help us get fruit from the spiny chonta tree that is impossible to climb. But when it comes to most things in life, the heart has the voice to listen to, because the heart knows how to follow the advice of the spirits. So I listen to my heart a lot, and I psychonavigate to the spirits themselves. I have faith in them and their desire to help us."

"How do you follow your heart?" Raul asked. "How can you be sure of what it says?"

"I listen." He lifted a cupped hand to his ear. "Your heart is part of the universe. If you listen to your heart, you hear the Voice of the Universe. We call it the Voice of the Universe or the Voice of the Soul. It speaks to us all the time. We only have to listen." He turned to me. "What do you hear?"

Everyone was still. Raul held the chicha gourd, poised just below his lips. I could hear only the fire and the sounds of life in the forests around us. Then I heard something, what I have been taught to call a "thought" but which really is a kind of voice. "I am told that I don't do this enough, don't listen. And that great wisdom is being spoken here tonight."

"You see?" Tampur slapped his knee. "Great wisdom is spoken every moment by the Voice of the Universe. You only need to listen. Your heart is always listening. Crossing your hands over your heart may help you to remember." Slowly he raised his hands and laid them across his heart. "Do this sometimes."

Ninety-year-old Shuar warrior and shaman who spoke of the Voice of the Universe.
PHOTOGRAPH BY THE AUTHOR.

He paused, listening, as each of us did the same. "See?" Tampur leaned over the fire. His toothless grin illuminated the night.

He sang us a song about the Voice of the Soul. Tayu had difficulty translating the actual words, although she told us that it honored ayahuasca as the Vine of the Soul that helped people become one with the plants and universe. "Ayahuasca," she interpreted, "allows us to die and be reborn; in this process, we clearly hear the Voice of the Universe, but more importantly, it opens our ears so we can always hear the Voice, whether we use ayahuasca or not."

I remembered the conversations with Viejo Itza that day on the pyramid—it seemed like a lifetime ago—and his comments about the plants opening us up, removing barriers such as fear. I decided not to bring up shapeshifting directly, but rather to focus on Tampur's beliefs,

Tuntuam drinking chicha. PHOTOGRAPH BY THE AUTHOR.

to try to discover how they might be similar to, or different from, Viejo Itza's. "Do you value trees beyond their healing powers and their uses for making houses, dugouts, and tools?"

Tampur launched into a discussion about the plant spirits. "They are the strongest," he concluded. "In my next life, I will be a tree, not a weak man. The trees give us the air we breathe, the water we drink, our very lives. What they provide as foods, canoes, spears, and the walls and roofing to our lodges is nothing compared to these other things. You know that air, water, earth, and fire are the Four Sacred Sisters, sacred because nothing can live without them. The Four Sisters cannot exist without forests. We cannot live without the forests. You cannot live without them! Your people way up there in the North cannot live without these trees." He shot me that grin of his. "I will be a tree."

Tayu turned to me. "Shouldn't we get more of his stories on tape?" I knew that for her, as for all of us, this was an important objective.

Tampur talked late into the night about his life as a warrior, a shaman, and a man who constantly tried to improve his ability to listen to the Voice and act accordingly. He described many of the warriors he had slain, detailing the battles themselves, the way the men had died, and the songs he had sung afterward, seeking the protection of the Voice of the Universe, asking for the strength he would need to follow his destiny. He sang these songs for us. We all drank a great deal of chicha.

I found my eyes often wandered to Tayu. Sitting quietly beside Tampur, in the firelight she looked gentle, serene, radiant. It occurred to me that my feelings toward her were not unlike those I felt toward the forest, a sunset, or a waterfall. On some level our spirits were united; I felt a sudden stab of guilt as I realized that the attraction was also sexual.

Suddenly Tampur stopped talking. He looked at me. Then at Tayu. "Well," he said, turning his body to face hers, "Enough of war. Let's discuss love." She glanced toward me—or was I imagining?—as she translated. Tampur's ancient voice fairly crackled with excited amusement as he told us about a Shuar ceremony held several times a year. Men and women would line up on opposite sides of the lodge. The men would beat drums and the women keep the rhythm by shaking dance belts strung with beads and shells that hung about their hips. The lines would move toward each other and away. People would shift positions. As the night wore on, couples would form—liaisons between people who might be married, but not to each other—and disappear together into the forest. In the morning, husbands and wives would reunite; the night would be accepted, all forgiven.

"A wonderful custom," Tampur observed when he had finished. "Solves many problems before they happen."

Finally, well after midnight, we all went to bed. I was careful to position my sleeping bag between Ehud's and Raul's. Tayu lay down on the other side of the fire.

Although exhausted, I could not sleep. I had an image of Tayu sitting in the firelight beside Tampur. She stood up to dance in front of me. She wore the traditional dance belt; beads and shells swayed with her hips. Then she began to fade. I heard a voice, stern and masculine. Tayu's image dissolved into that of a man in a black suit, poised before television cameras. "To avoid temptation," he said, " I never allow myself to ride in a car with a woman, unless someone else is present. Never. Not even my secretary. I never have lunch alone with a woman." I recognized the voice, but could not place it.

I sat up. The fire was burning brightly. I looked around. They all appeared to be asleep. I wished Tayu would wake up, look my way, speak. I longed to hear her voice. Then I remembered. I heard that male voice

again and this time with it came the face. Billy Graham. Being inter-
viewed on national television about Jim Bakker. How, the reporter had
asked the Reverend Graham, did he guard against temptation?

I lay back down, relieved to have identified the image. The glow of the
fire reflected in the thatching overhead. Perhaps Billy Graham had it right:
maybe he was speaking directly to me. Avoid situations that tempt. I con-
gratulated myself for sleeping across the fire from Tayu. I closed my eyes.

Then I saw Tayu's face floating above me. Her gentle expression gave
me cause to rethink, to reconsider. Why should I congratulate myself on
avoiding her? She was a wonderful human being, a powerful teacher, a
sister. My reaction had grown out of another feeling, an insidious one—
guilt. Graham's words struck me as the tools of a manipulative culture
that played upon guilt in order to control others. Never alone with a
woman! What did it take to say such a thing? It was an attitude that divided people, the genders, just as the scientific system divided species
and the business community set nature aside, as something apart. How
long could we continue separating ourselves like that and continue to
survive?

Then I thought about the story of Eve and the serpent. Evil woman,
evil nature. Where do such ideas come from? What is it within our culture that erects those barriers, that represses the natural and prohibits us
from honoring our most nurturing aspects? And what is it that makes us
think we must impose these ideas and values on to others?

Realizing that I needed sleep, that these questions would not be answered during the night, I forced my thoughts to change, to slow down,
move away from the questioning. I searched for a vision that would be
conducive to sleeping and returned to Tampur's story about love, the
celebration, the men and women coming together for a night of sharing.
Images swam before me. Like phantoms, they materialized out of the
forest—Shuar people of all ages lining up for an ecstatic ritual. I was
only mildly surprised to see my own face superimposed over both lines
of dancers, men and women. I felt peaceful, contented.

I fell asleep. I was aware of the crackling fire, the forests surrounding
me, Tampur and his family, Tayu, the night . . . yet I was sound asleep, as
though the barriers between wakefulness and sleep had disintegrated.

At some point I found myself fully awake and sitting up. I felt a pulling, as though the jungle were calling me. The embers of the fire told me that I must have slept for several hours. I glanced at Tayu. No movement whatsoever. I lay down, nestling deep into my sleeping bag, and told myself it was just my imagination. Then I remembered the Voice of the Soul, the Voice of the Universe. The question occurred to me: What is imagination anyway? Is it simply a word we use instead of *voice?*

I struggled out of the sleeping bag, onto my feet. The lodge was dark except for the embers of the fire. A dog raised his head and whimpered at me. Then he returned to sleep. Everything else was quiet.

I walked outside. The sky was alive with stars. A firefly flickered here and there among the trees. I realized that I had neglected to bring my flashlight; I was reluctant to go back for it and run the risk of inciting the dog to wake the others. I thought I knew where the trail lay and, in any case, the stars enabled me to see the silhouetted tops of the jungle canopy. Slowly I walked into the night, feeling drawn by some force I could not identify. I crossed my hands over my heart and knew that I was on the right path.

The sounds of the jungle night seemed louder than I had remembered them in the past, as though they were the chorus for the Voice. I tried to imagine the bodies that produced each. In my mind's eye I saw frogs, toads, insects of various sizes and shapes, nighthawks and owls, a small ocelot and the glowing eyes of a large cat. I slowed a bit, but continued on through the forest.

The trees suddenly parted and I found myself in a clearing. I froze. A blue light flashed high up in the top of the canopy. And again. Then it rose out of the forest—a vibrating globe of blue light, like the one I had seen during the journey I had taken on the Mayan pyramid with Viejo Itza. It hovered just above the treetops. Then another light appeared. This one seemed to materialize out of thin air. The two hovered side by side. Like huge balls of energy, they moved closer to me and then flashed quickly away, disappearing behind the thick wall of the rainforest trees.

I stood there for what seemed a very long time, hoping they would return and at the same time trembling with anxiety. My body felt energized and drained all at once. I had a vivid memory of that day on the Mayan pyramid with Viejo Itza, of melting into the ball of energy that had turned from gold to blue and grown from the size of a grapefruit until its diameter had become as large as I am tall, of Viejo Itza instructing me to use the stone he had given me as a sort of tool, allowing it to move around and touch the ball of energy, and finally, hearing what I now knew as the Voice of my Soul tell me in answer to my question that my desire to shapeshift into a ball of energy was a dream, not a fantasy. This experience seemed like the realization of that dream. My mind told me to run toward the lights, but something held me back. I knew they were gone. And I also had a certainty I would experience them again. Finally I turned and hurried back to Tampur's lodge. I stole a last look in the direction of the blue globes. Not a sign.

Nothing had changed. The dog raised his head as I walked in; his tail thumped the floor in friendly recognition. I climbed back into my sleeping bag and sat for a while studying the glowing embers.

Later that night I had a dream. At least I think it was a dream, although the next day when I told him about it, Raul suggested that it might have been more than a dream. I was gliding slowly through the sky, surrounded by shimmering blue light, looking down on a desert. Men with animals moved across the sand. From time to time one of them would look up and point at me. They were following me. I felt warm, ecstatic. I was aware that this had been going on for many days. Below me I saw a town. At its outskirts was a small cave. I came to a stop above it. A light within the cave illuminated a group of people and animals and a newborn child. The men who had followed me entered the shed. I moved higher into the sky, to a position where I could see the vast land, the town, and the cave. A circle of golden light radiated from the place where the child was sleeping.

I awoke to the sounds of laughter. All was dark. As my eyes adjusted I saw forms crawling near the embers of the fire. Someone shuffled logs, blew air, and the fire came to life. Birds sang, a chorus of them, and the night became morning, a hazy filtered light. The laughter grew louder. I sat up. The whole Shuar family was on the floor: infants, children, adults, even Tampur. They were romping with each other and playing with a small animal that might have been a monkey.

Raul sat up next to me. "They never grow out of childhood," he said. "A Shuar elder once told me that evening is the time for the old people to teach about history and traditions, and morning is for the children to teach about playing."

We rolled up our sleeping bags and made ready to leave for Kapawi, where Jaime awaited us. While Raul and Tayu prepared breakfast, I found myself alone with Tampur and his teenage great-grandson, who spoke Spanish as well as Shuar. We walked together outside the lodge. I took the opportunity to tell Tampur about the blue globes in the sky.

As he listened, he nodded his head and grinned with pleasure. When I had finished, he said one word which needed no translation: "Kitiar."

"Kitiar?" I asked, astonished. "That was Kitiar?"

He nodded enthusiastically. "Kitiar."

"They weren't extraterrestials? From another planet? A star?"

"Yes, yes," he said. "Kitiar." He waved his hands over his head. "Other planets. Jungle spirits. Kitiar." He patted my back.

Then a thought came to me, a question. "You knew that I was Kitiar's friend?" He nodded. "How?"

He pointed in the direction where the blue globes had been the night before. "We are all one," he said. I told him about the incident with the bat—how Kitiar had predicted it, that I had seen it while Kitiar was healing me, and then the way it had appeared on the night when Kitiar vanished. "Yes," he said matter-of-factly. "Kitiar became the bat. Now blue globes. What he is, he is." Then he paused and again patted my back. "Do not think so much." His hands went to my heart.

We stood there for awhile. The sounds of the waking jungle filled the air. Looking off and up toward the treetops, he spoke slowly. "We old Shuar are able to become trees and animals. We know that whenever there is a fierce storm we must bend like the palm rather than being uprooted like a stiff old tree. Shamans change form and use it against their adversaries." He turned to me. "Learn to be the globe of energy. Like your teacher, Kitiar."

Chapter 15

Indigenous Elders Speak Out

During breakfast I told Raul and Ehud about the blue globes. Raul grew very excited. "Jaime saw them a couple of weeks ago in Kapawi, where we'll be tonight."

I was incredulous. "The same—are you sure?"

"I think so. But we'll be with him in a few hours. He can tell us himself." I felt relieved, vindicated, as though Jaime's sighting was a confirmation that I had not just imagined them.

We thanked our hosts and hauled our packs to the airstrip. There was not a breath of air; already it was unusually hot. We piled everything under the lean-to where we had drunk chicha the previous day.

I sat in the shade, absorbed by memories of the night before. A gang of children exploded from the forest and came running toward us.

"They heard the plane," Raul said, shaking his head incredulously. "No matter how hard I strain my ears, they always hear it before me."

It circled once to make sure that we were there and then came swooping in to land on the rutted airstrip, a landing that threatened to shake every rivet from its fuselage. We dragged our packs across the heat-drenched airstrip and climbed into the plane. However, when the pilot pushed the button to start the engine, it refused to turn over. He tried and tried, but nothing happened.

"Battery!" he exclaimed, slamming a fist against the side of his seat.

Then he pushed open his door, fumbled in a box beneath his seat, and broke into a smile. "Thank the Good Lord," he beamed. "The Virgin accompanies us. I have the rope!" He held up a long strand of thick manila line, like the type used to tie a yacht to a dock. "Everybody out. We'll jump-start her."

I thought he must be joking, until he began to wind the rope around the propeller shaft. Ehud unpacked his video camera and filmed him.

The pilot lined us all up at a right angle to the plane—all except Ehud, who had gained the pilot's unspoken permission to continue with his filming. We each held tightly to the rope. We were about to start an airplane engine the same way I used to start an old outboard motor as a young boy on a New Hampshire lake: by cranking the flywheel with a rope! It seemed preposterous.

We strained against the rope. As we threw our combined weight into it, amazingly the shaft began to turn. Very slowly at first, until we broke the inertia. Then we raced away from the plane with the rope across our shoulders and heard the explosion as the engine fired. We stood gasping for breath and watched the propeller flash sunlight back into our eyes.

When finally airborne I found myself questioning my sanity. Why had I taken off in this crippled plane? What if the engine decided to cut out now?

Then I felt suddenly calm. Looking down on the treetops, I was taken by their ancient majesty. The tallest had been there for hundreds of years. I remembered stories from *The Tales of King Arthur and His Court* that my grandmother used to read to me as a child. A big old book with frayed pages that had been shared by several generations on my father's side of the family, it contained wonderful color illustrations. As if the book lay open in my lap, I recalled one of the scenes of Sir Galahad riding through an enchanted forest on a magnificent charger. Sunlight slanted through the trees. Both he and the horse were draped in red. He was looking up at an image that seemed to shimmer with the intensity of the hazy blue light surrounding it. It was the Holy Grail. I was totally awed by this picture and returned to the book to study it often. There was something personal about the Grail as it hovered above the trees, something that seemed to call to me, as though it and I were connected. A thought returned to me that might have dated back to my childhood, that might perhaps have accompanied the sound of my grandmother's voice. It was almost more a feeling than a thought, a creation of the heart rather than the mind, that all of life is a quest. Like the knights of the Round Table, who I had come to know in my childhood, I was on a grand adventure seeking something divine.

"You saw those blue globes, too?" Jaime asked after we landed in Kapawi. I sensed that he was as relieved as I had been to learn that someone else had witnessed them.

His experience had been similar to mine. The globes had hovered quietly near him and then departed. Afterward he remembered having powerful dreams, although when he awoke he could not recall any of the details.

We were interrupted by shouting. A group of Achuar men and women had circled around Tayu. They sounded like angry bees defending the hive.

We ran to the edge of the circle. Two men were standing very close to Tayu. One shoved her. Jaime rushed in. He wrapped an arm about her shoulders and, thrusting his hand into the air, shouted something. Then he turned abruptly to the man who had shoved her and spoke to him.

The Achuar backed off. The other man made a little speech to the crowd. Jaime waved his arms at them. Another spoke, an older man who had been quiet until them. The men and women broke apart, although they did not go far.

The older man said something to Jaime in a stern voice. The words were Achuar. Jaime turned to the one who had pushed Tayu; he stood apart, looking contrite. Jaime's voice was soothing. Suddenly the one who had pushed Tayu smiled and, stepping next to Jaime, translated into Spanish the words the elder had spoken. "She is Shuar, our enemy. We will kill her, unless she flies on this plane back to her people."

Raul stepped up beside Tayu. He argued that she should stay, pointing out that she was our translator.

"I speak Spanish. I will translate for you," the Achuar man insisted. "She just came from Tampur's. He killed my father." The man struck himself on the chest. "She cannot remain here, alive."

Jaime took Tayu, Raul, and me aside. "You are my sister," he said

to her. "But sadly I think you should leave. If you stay, your lif_
danger. Strange things are happening around here. These people are
very frightened."

Tayu's departure left me with an empty, sad feeling. I watched the plane
disappear into the tree line, and I wondered what she was thinking. I
thought about balance. We were men without women—at least without
women we could relate to. Although there were Achuar women all around
us, I did not feel close to them. They appeared to be my enemies. After
all, I too had just come from Tampur's! Men without women, the shamans say, are either men at war or men out of balance.

Jaime led us through the jungle away from the airstrip. All of us were
in a somber mood. Raul and Ehud began a conversation about Latin
American history and the role the church had played. As much to take
my mind off Tayu as out of curiosity, I asked Jaime why the Achuar were
frightened.

"There is constant rumor of war between Ecuador and Peru over oil,
John. People hear gunshots along the border all the time. And then . . ."
He paused and looked me in the eye. "We've been friends a long time. I
tell you this not to hurt you, but because it is the way I see it. Your people
put terrible pressures on the Achuar."

I asked who it was he called "my people" and what sort of pressures he
referred to.

He clasped a big hand on my shoulder. "Your people are gringos,
brother, and they pressure these Achuar to cut and destroy their forests.
The oil companies north of here have all but wiped out the Waorani,
Cofan, and Secoya. They've done irreparable damage to the forests, na-
palmed thousands of hectares, polluted the rivers, and caused epidemics
of previously unknown diseases. The Achuar have watched this happen."
Then he turned and hugged me. When we pulled apart, his eyes met
mine. "Of course, I know you are not one of them. I know that."

"Thank you," I said, forcing a smile.

We walked on. After a while he continued. "The Achuar have difficulty living off the land. Like the Shuar, their population has skyrock-
eted. The forests are being cut all around them. They have a very serious
problem here. Hunting and gathering as a way of life is over. They know

they will be seduced and blackmailed into opening roads for oil and gold companies, for mahogany and other precious woods. They need money. One of the reasons I wanted you to come is so you can listen to their problems and perhaps find a way to assist them."

We emerged into a clearing. "The Achuar," Jaime continued, "are not looking for handouts. They want to do their share. They believe they have many things to teach the rest of us."

Walking through the sunlight we arrived at a small lake. Groups of Achuar men were digging holes along the shore and positioning large poles in them. "I believe it too," Jaime said. "They have so much knowledge about the plants, spirituality, loving the earth, each other—the foundations for a new sort of school, perhaps. Where they will teach our people about ourselves." He pointed toward the holes. "This lodge, when finished, will be very comfortable for North Americans and Europeans—good food, safe drinking water—yet it will also belong to the Achuar. It will be a place where outsiders can feel secure and at the same time live as one with the rainforest."

Jaime reminded me that Ecuadorian businessmen had invested over $1 million into the lodge. "They did it," he said "in good faith and based only on what I told them. Most have never been here." He sighed. "Perhaps they'll never come." He swung his hands in a circle, indicating the area where the men were working. "The architecture and materials are Achuar—not a nail in the place. I simply help them understand certain things that gringos will want, if they are to come here. All the workers are Achuar. They own the lodge; the investors only hold a lease on it, giving them the right to use it for fifteen years."

"But they have expectations."

"The investors? Oh . . . of course. They expect a decent rate of return. Yet I think they also are in this for the hope it offers. After all, there are safer ways to make a rate of return." He stopped. "I have faith," he said after a pause. "To change the world we must change the dream. We must have faith."

"Jaime," I said at last. "What is it you expect of me? How can I assist these people?"

He smiled. "Only listen. And watch. Open your ears and eyes—all your senses. Dream. And remember what you learn. You will know."

I had to laugh. "That simple?"

He gave me a look. "It is all I can ask."

We walked on in silence. For some reason, a passage from the Bhagavad Gita came to me. *He lives in wisdom who sees himself in all and all in him. He is forever free who has broken out of the ego cage of* I *and* mine. I repeated it for Jaime.

He nodded solemnly. "A wise book."

I summarized Tampur's conversation about the Four Sacred Sisters. "The Bhagavad Gita describes a voice within all of us that tells us each the same thing: What we want is not money, fame, or material possessions, but a world of peace, hearts filled with love, and an earth where the air and water are clean, the environment healthy. We want to rid ourselves of those unwanted habits and negative thoughts that prohibit us from living in peace with ourselves, the environment, and our neighbors."

We spent the afternoon wandering around the area and into the jungle. Then, just before sunset, we took a dugout up a tributary of the Pastaza River to a place where Amazonian freshwater dolphins frequently congregate to fish and play. We drifted for perhaps half an hour looking and waiting for them. None showed up on this particular day. "It happens like this," Jaime explained. "That is part of nature. Sometimes they're here, sometimes they're not. We will have no cages or fences. For our visitors to see wildlife, it must be part of the animals' dream as well as that of the tourists."

Two days later we were invited to have dinner with a group of Achuar elders who made community decisions. We were told that they had been gathering since our arrival; several had traveled long distances to meet with us.

Late in the afternoon, the four of us were escorted into the community meeting hall. Perhaps two dozen men—elders all—sat along the walls. Our translator walked us around and introduced us to each individually. Then we, too, were given stools.

Several of the elders made welcoming speeches, each one standing and facing us as he did so. The language, as well as the presentation, was formal. Jaime took the floor and introduced us. He explained that Raul was his partner in the ecotourism business that had arranged for the financing of the lodge they were currently building, that I was a writer whose message is carried to many countries in a variety of languages, and that Ehud was a publisher whose books influence millions of people on many continents.

He touched each of us on the top of the head. "They come to offer their help and to seek your wisdom."

The meeting then was opened for general discussion. Women entered with bowls of chicha. The atmosphere became less formal.

Many of the elders spoke, addressing us directly. Despite the earlier formalities, I was impressed with their willingness to open their hearts to us. Almost every one of them wanted to describe the dilemma facing their people. Their story was as Jaime had portrayed it. During the last ten years they had experienced changes like nothing that had ever before happened to the Achuar. Although the religious and medical missions had at first seemed to bring many benefits, now they were not so sure these were all that beneficial.

"More of our babies live," one old warrior said. "More of us have longer lives. But we are threatened with starvation. We cannot feed our families by hunting—too many people, too little game. We must get down on our knees and beg for handouts." He glanced around defiantly. "This is not the Achuar way. The white man has made us his slave. He defeated us not with weapons, but with books and medicines."

Another told of how a group of Achuar had walked out of the jungle, up the Andes, and all the way to Quito to demand that the government recognize their rights to land that was being granted to colonists from the Andes. Joined by other indigenous people as well as college students and sympathizers, they had camped out in the central plaza until the President had heard their case. They thought their perseverance had been rewarded after the government granted the Achuar title to one million acres. "We celebrated when our people returned with fancy papers," the elder said. "Then, months later, we were told our title is no good if the big companies find oil or gold on our land. They can destroy it if they want—just like in the North, with the Waorani and the Cofan."

My heart went out to them as they spoke about the conflicts the white men had created in individuals as well as the greater culture. "What do we say to our young people when they are offered rifles and radios?" one of them asked. "Should they not have the things your young people have? But at what cost? These appear to be gifts, yet in our hearts we know that strangers do not offer gifts like these without expecting something in return."

When he sat down another stood, a decrepit old man who used a long stick to help him get to his feet. "Pretty soon the gift-givers return and ask permission to cut this elder tree here and then that one over there. Our young people want more gifts so they agree. 'What is an old tree?' they ask. 'We need to modernize,' they say. 'Our babies need to be vaccinated. They require food that the jungle can no longer offer.' What do we reply to these young people?"

All we could do was listen and then, after they had finished, tell them that we had heard their pain and that our hearts cried. "Not only for the Achuar," I added. "Also for the Waorani, the Cofan, and the Shuar—both your friends and enemies. And my own people, the white man, for I believe that we are one of the unhappiest cultures on earth. We are headed down a path that leads us off a cliff and we are taking everybody else with us. Not just people, but many other species too. This is tragic."

Ehud emphasized that people throughout the world were struggling with similar problems. He described the plight of Australian Aborigines, the Dyaks of Borneo, and the Tibetans. And he assured them that the Achuar's story would be heard.

I suggested that we needed their assistance as much as they needed ours. "My people must learn to love the sacred elements." I talked about the idea of partnership, describing it as a bridge where help, knowledge, compassion, and energy travel in both directions. A thought struck me. "We need a way of changing the collective dream of those who have caused so much damage—my people." I promised to return to the US and try to organize a new partnership to work with them. "I cannot promise you I will succeed. Only that I will try."

Then I had another thought. I looked directly at the old man with the long stick. "Help me find a way to give your young people gifts—or money—when they decide *not* to cut that old tree."

Slowly, leaning heavily on the cane, he once again stood up. His eyes met mine. "We do not own these forests. They belong to no man and to all men." He glanced down at his cane. "We use them for many things." He tapped the cane. "Always with their permission. We honor and respect each tree. We know the forests are much older than we and that they will outlive all of us. By cutting them in your selfish, disrespectful ways, your people may cause all people to leave this wonderful Mother Earth. But the forests will endure. You will not destroy them." He paused, looking around. "You ask us to help you find ways to pay our people for not cutting. Well, we must answer that this is not even a question. What is it you ask? Surely you know that you in the North cannot live without these trees. You will have no air to breathe, no water to drink, no life. Yet it is your people who come here offering our people piles of paper money if only they will cut this elder tree here or all those elder trees over there. What for? We don't know. Sometimes your people haul the trees away, down the rivers. Sometimes you just burn them and then bring in huge towers that reach to the heavens and stick their long stingers deep, deep into Mother Earth until she bleeds black blood. Why? Who can tell? All we elders know is that these people of yours are evil, black magicians. Now you are here. Our friend Jaime says you are a friend. We believe him. You ask: How can we help you pay our young not to sell the trees, that they do not even own, to your black magicians?"

He grunted and the suggestion of a smile crossed his wizened face. "Easy. Simply pay us to protect them from your own destructive people. Pay us to assure that your babies will have air and water. Shapeshift your people." He eased himself back down onto his stool.

During the next several days we hiked in the forests and took short canoe trips along the rivers, learning as much as we could about the Achuar, their knowledge of the plants and animals, and their ways of perceiving the world. The experience was fascinating, and yet tainted for me by the suspicion that we were sharing the last moment of a tradition that stretched back to a time before all recorded history. I felt honored to be participating in the lives of these people; however, I was deeply saddened by the knowledge that soon they would be exposed to the materialism that held such a self-destructive grip on my own culture.

Then one morning it was time to leave Kapawi. We carried our packs down to the river and loaded them into a huge dugout canoe, one that measured over fifty feet long. We were headed for an Achuar shaman's house that was many hours upriver, in a community that had seldom been visited by outsiders. We were warned that many of the people we would meet had never seen a white person. There was no telling how they would react to us.

When we began our journey up the river we had perhaps thirty passengers and were loaded with many baskets of various goods. As we progressed, we dropped people off at little paths into the forest. They all worked at Jaime's site and returned home periodically to bring supplies and help out with the family's chores. Eventually most of them would find their way back to Kapawi.

I noticed that the further upriver we progressed, the more timid were the people. At first it was only the children who turned heel and ran as soon as they spotted Jaime, Ehud, Raul, and me. Then it was the old people too. But once we had passed a certain point, everyone hid from us. When I asked Jaime about this, he told me that those who had not seen whites before were terrified by our appearance. "One of their legends," he explained, "is about the 'Evias,' giant white cannibals who ate the Achuar. Even their most valiant warriors were powerless against them. Eventually the Evias were destroyed by Etsáa, the sun god. But now the people wonder if some of the Evias didn't survive. That would be us."

I realized that all four of us towered over the Achuar, whose average height, for males, I would guess to be at about 5 feet 6 inches. I kept silent, although I wanted to ask the obvious question: Aren't we in fact the cannibals their legend predicted, who devour not only their forests and culture but also threaten the survival of our entire species?

It was an incredible trip through some of the most spectacular rainforests I had ever seen. We counted many species—mostly birds—that are on the official endangered species list. The air was often filled with butterflies. As sun and rain alternated, we witnessed the births and deaths of numerous rainbows. Eyes peered out at us from the water and the jungle.

We arrived at the shaman's lodge shortly before sunset. It sat high up on a bank overlooking the river. The traditional oval-shaped lodge was huge and majestic, the most palatial indigenous home I had ever seen. We estimated it at one hundred feet in length, with an intricately thatched roof that must have reached three to four stories high at the center. The children scattered as we approached, racing off into the jungle.

The shaman himself, Tsukanka, was younger than I had expected, perhaps in his early forties. There was no question about his authority. His own people stepped back from him as he came up to shake our hands. We could feel his power, his *arutam*, the spirit that sets warriors apart. Here was a man who did not fear to do battle—neither against human nor spiritual enemies. His eyes were piercing. He spoke no Spanish, yet I knew we would not have any difficulty communicating.

Several dozen people were invited into his lodge for the evening ceremony. I guessed the word had spread that we were not the dreaded Evias. Or perhaps they came to watch Tsukanka demolish the giant white cannibals. Outside the sun lingered along the horizon, but inside it was dark. We laid out our sleeping bags along a wall that had been designated as the guest area. I could feel the Achuar as they studied us intently, especially the children. Some dashed up to touch us, then scurried away.

The shaman sat on a stool in the center of his great lodge. Framed by the fire that crackled in front of him, he swayed from side to side as if touched by an invisible wind. Suddenly the activity ceased. All went quiet. Even the children settled down. It was uncanny. No signal had been given, yet everything was still; not a soul uttered a sound.

Tsukanka called us to him. He pointed at me and then at a stool beside the fire. I sat down. By the light of the flames I could see in his hands a small stone that reminded me of the one Viejo Itza had given to me. He breathed into it and chanted softly. Then he handed it to me. I spoke to it in English, asking it to help me shapeshift into a globe of energy, like the ones I had visualized at the pyramid in the Yucatan and had seen that night at Tampur's. I handed it back to him. He nodded solemnly, as though he understood.

He dropped the stone into a small gourd and chanted softly. The sounds were deep and guttural. They brought to me the image of a jaguar mating—half-growl, half-purr. He lifted the gourd in both his hands to his heart. The chanting grew louder for an instant and then ceased. He handed me the gourd.

I drank the dark liquid. The stone bumped against my teeth. I let it rest there and touched its smooth surface with my tongue.

Chapter 16

Shapeshifting Through Time and Space

I wandered outside. The night was unusually dark; not a single star was visible in the sky.

I knew that I had imbibed a mild form of ayahuasca. It tasted different from the ayahuasca I had taken several times with the Shuar—not nearly as bitter or potent. I was quite certain that I would not vomit, as is customary with the stronger doses.

Raul joined me. "Different," he said.

We stood silent at the edge of the dark mass of trees that held back the jungle. Inside the lodge, Tsukanka began to chant. Then I heard the hiss of a snake. I jumped back, only to realize that it had been Raul sucking in his breath. He pointed into the heavens.

My eyes followed his finger to a star. It was very large, the only one visible. It held me. I felt his arm around my shoulders. The star was strobing: green, blue, red.

"Incredible!" Raul squeezed my shoulders. It appeared to move toward us.

We stood for a long time watching it. "It seems to speak," he said at one point. "I think I see it as a face." A little later he asked if it was anything like the blue globes. I could only reply that in appearance it was not. I lost all track of time and of everything else except the star, which continued to strobe. Finally it appeared to move closer to us and then away, losing its magic and becoming just another of the millions of brilliant entities that ignited the night.

Ehud came out from the lodge to join us. The three of us stood together in the night. "That was wonderful chanting," Ehud said. It struck me that Tsukanka was quiet now.

"I think the shaman is taking a break," Ehud observed. He suggested we walk along the river. He told us that Jaime had fallen asleep.

I had an impulse to return to the lodge. I declined his offer to walk by the river, but urged them to go on alone. "I don't think any of us needs babysitting. That ayahuasca was about as strong as a half bowl of chicha." We all laughed.

After they disappeared I remained in the little clearing around the lodge. I stared up into the tops of the trees. They took on the appearance of giant heads with fluffy hair silhouetted against the starlit sky. Perhaps, I thought with a chuckle, they arrived in the blue globes, centuries ago. Tsukanka resumed his chanting and it was as though the trees were speaking through him to me. *We are here to help you,* they seemed to say. *When you need energy or advice, come to us.*

I recalled Kitiar talking about the tree spirits. Had he not said something about arriving from Pleiades? I thought about the way Tampur had described Kitiar: "Other planets. Jungle spirits. Kitiar," he had said. The feelings I was experiencing reminded me of an ayahuasca trip and yet I was very aware of my physical presence in a way that was not at all similar to the other times I had taken it.

I turned and entered the lodge. The fire had died to a pile of embers. I stood just inside the doorway, allowing my eyes to adjust. I began to make out a movement that I sensed was directed at me. It was several yards from where the fire smoldered, a slow wave, like an arm rising and falling. I went to it.

Tsukanka was still sitting on his stool. Although his face was hidden in shadows, I knew he was smiling. "Lie down," he seemed to say, without the use of his voice.

I felt my way onto a straw mat that had been placed in front of him. I stretched out on my back, the hard-packed earth beneath me. I thought I could feel the earth's energy flowing into me. Tsukanka began to chant softly.

A warm breeze passed across me. I was very relaxed. A sense of well-being enveloped me. He laid a hand over my eyes. Words came to me, through his chanting. "Your ancestors were shamans; every one comes from a shamanic culture," the words said, although even as I heard them I understood the absurdity of the situation. The words were in English. But I could not deny the words—they had been spoken, whether they originated from Tsukanka or someplace else. I thought about them. It was certainly true that if we go back far enough into our ancestry, we all come from shamanic cultures. It does not matter where we trace our heritage back to—Africa, Asia, Europe, the Middle East—we all have shamans in our lineage. They are part of our genes, our DNA, our cellular makeup.

This raised a question for me. I knew I should ask it, yet I hesitated, embarrassed by the thought of speaking to this man in English or Spanish. Then I remembered a night with Kitiar, an incredible psychonavigational journey I thought I was taking alone, only to learn in the morning that he had been with me the whole time. It was outlandish, even unbelievable. Yet his descriptions of our journey together left no doubt. After I wrote about it in *The World Is As You Dream It*, I received letters confirming that others who had worked with shamans in Tibet and Indonesia had experienced similar shared journeys. If that had happened, then anything seemed possible. I felt Tsukanka's hands on my eyelids, and decided to ask.

"If we all come from shamanic cultures, what happened? Why did we give up that dream? Why did we replace this earth-honoring way of life with the commercialism and materialism that is now destroying our species?"

I felt his lips touch my ear. He was chanting directly into me. The sound was like the wind in the leaves As he pressed his hands down on my eyes, I saw one of the blue globes. It hovered above me.

I was shocked by its presence. Yet it also was somehow expected, as if I had been awaiting it, knowing this moment would arrive, that a part of me had intended it. I was amazed and, at the same time, accepting of what I was experiencing. Feelings flooded me, sweeping over me in waves of indescribable emotion. I remember thinking that all of it, especially my feelings, were beyond description. This was an event that was so out of context with what I have been taught is possible that to this day I have difficulty expressing it in words.

In this heightened state I reached a level where my intellect was very clear, where despite the overwhelming passions I felt, I knew exactly what was occurring and what my role was. I understood that I was supposed to enter the globe. I could see its energy field shimmering around it, as though inviting me in. I felt at peace. I also knew that I was filled with power, that my energy was exactly the same as the energy field I was watching. I remember letting out a long breath, releasing myself into this new reality.

Then I too was hovering. I moved through the air effortlessly—across the lodge, through the doorway, and up over the dark forest canopy.

The thought came to me that although I might never be able to explain this moment, it was absolutely real. As lucid as the canoe trip earlier in the day. It was the opposite of being in a dream and knowing that you are dreaming. This was happening to me physically, on a cellular level. I knew it. I was absolutely certain that I was not dreaming, hallucinating, or imagining, and understood that, although I knew it, I might never convince anyone else that it had happened. I had shapeshifted into a globe of energy. I had been transformed in the most basic way. My body had merged with that of another. Incredibly, the sensation seemed completely natural.

The globe—me—cast a strong light all around. The forest below was illuminated. I studied it carefully. I could pick out individual trees. I spied a nocturnal rodent scurrying through the underbrush. Then everything went blurry for an instant, like fast forwarding a video. Just as suddenly, it returned to normal. Looking down, I approached a river and caught a flash of movement. There on the bank was a band of soldiers. I was surprised to see that they wore armor—ancient helmets, breast plates, and shields. Their faces had Asiatic features. In their darkly polished metal and plumed helmets, they looked totally out of place. Suddenly they let out bloodcurdling screams and, brandishing swords, charged into a cave in the river bank. I let myself descend to a better vantage point. After a short interval they emerged, dragging terrified women and children from the dark mouth of the cave, their armor smeared with gore. Their leader unfurled a banner emblazoned with a rampant, fire-breathing dragon.

He cupped his hands to his mouth and shouted: "For the Emperor, we civilize you."

Then the oddest thing happened. He glanced up at me. His mouth dropped open. He staggered and fell to his knees. But quickly he recovered and hustled his men, along with their captives, back inside the cave, casting furtive glances at me as he herded them in.

I understood that I not only had shifted into a sort of unidentified flying object that could be seen by people, but that I had also transported myself into another time.

My vision went blurry again. When it returned I was above a huge circular stone building. It was open at the top so I could look down and see bleachers filled with cheering spectators. The middle area was a field, like a football stadium. A group of women and children huddled together in the center. Three men moved away from them toward a large wooden door at one end of the open space. Their eyes fixed on the door, the three men crouched like combatants preparing to fight. I realized that they were intent on protecting the women and children from some terrible menace that lurked behind the door. I could actually smell the terror of all the people in that little group. Both contestants and spectators concentrated so intently on the activities that no one saw me. Suddenly the spectators rose to their feet. The door swung open. Four lions burst into the arena and charged the three men. "Civilize the barbarians!" the crowd shouted in unison.

I pulled up rapidly, not wanting to see the slaughter I knew would follow. The coliseum fell away below me, until it became a mere speck.

After that, event followed event. They came rapidly, yet each was absolutely real. Since my descriptions cannot possibly do them justice, I will merely summarize a few of them, enough to provide a frame for the final canvas, the thirteen women who answered my original question. I will say that during the entire journey there was never a doubt in my mind that I was observing living, physical beings involved in true-life situations.

I found myself looking down on a bustling market. A long caravan of camels and horses entered it. People came running in to the market from all around to gawk at the exotic goods that had obviously been bought or pirated from cultures far away. I moved on. At a nearby port, sailing ships unloaded a cargo of human beings. I dropped lower for a better look. A tattered line of men, women, and children shuffled along a wooden wharf. They were prodded on by men in leather aprons who periodically cracked whips across their naked backs. Chained together, they were tortured, humiliated, despondent human beings who had lost the will to live. Sounds of despair and the smell of excrement permeated the air.

I saw many things as I journeyed on through the ancient world that showed men dominating other men and women and children. In every case, those in control were from cultures that have been defined in history books as the most advanced. I was fascinated by everything I witnessed, yet after a while I began to feel sickened by the gore. At one point I felt certain I would vomit.

Immediately I found myself in more modern times, observing scenes of a different type of horror: huge scars in the earth where emaciated people mined gems and minerals, gigantic factories belching pollution into the atmosphere, children in sweatshops, women working on assembly lines, women selling their bodies on ghetto street corners, stores as big as cathedrals filled with shoppers who appeared to take no joy in shopping, slums packed along hillsides in crowded cities, families living next to open sewers in cardboard boxes and opulent mansions high above the ocean. Sometimes the people I watched also saw me. Usually, however, they were too preoccupied. Those who did notice reacted with shock and fear, although I did nothing to threaten them.

Then I was moving across green hills. The sun was shining and the grasses were swaying in the breeze. I could smell freshness in the air. The place felt altogether different from the others I had experienced. I came over a rise and saw a little valley below where a group of people had assembled—all women, dressed in black, who stood in a formal group, as though posing for a photograph in the late 1800s. There were thirteen of them altogether.

I descended for a closer look. Each of the women held a tall, pointed sowing stick; at their feet was a garden of dead plants and grotesque stumps, a sight that struck me as completely foreign to this place where green abounded.

One of them looked up and pointed. They all spotted me and smiled, as though they had been awaiting my arrival. Unlike the others, they appeared unafraid. The one who had seen me first beckoned for me to join them. They formed a circle and I drifted slowly into the middle of it. They gave off a scent like that of sweet herbs.

"Your question?" the first asked. "The one about why your culture abandoned shamanic, earth-honoring ways . . . remember?" She nodded at me. "Of course you do. Well, the answer revolves around the idea of domination. But that word wasn't the one voiced. Instead they used other words, such as . . .

The twelve women chimed in, a chorus of shrill voices: "Progress, advances, civilization."

"You see, the rich always wanted to get richer, consolidate their power." Again the chorus: "Take control."

"Hu*man* history—massive movements toward centralization."

The chorus: "Advanced states, culture, higher standards of living."

"Technology."

"Control."

The one who spoke alone turned in a slow circle. "You asked, so we are here to explain. But you've already seen it. Or at least enough. There is a direct correlation between the rise of 'advanced, civilized societies' and the demise of shamanic ones that emphasize closeness to and dependence on nature. That encourage ecstasy."

"Ecstasy!" The women rolled their eyes and moved their bodies seductively; four or five of them touched their breasts.

"Ecstasy is what we all desire. It is a natural state of heightened passions when we feel our oneness with all things. But those who would dominate others hate ecstasy. Passion includes anger and rebellion. It threatens their control. They discredit shamans who espouse it. They try to force the goddess out of religion and the priestess out of women. Woman the ecstatic. Instead they teach their sheep that happiness comes from owning things, that heaven is a huge store. 'Out with the primitive,' they shout. 'Tame nature!' "

"Tame nature, tame nature," the women sang in a mocking chant. "Kill the shamans. Oooooh . . . Imprison sacred forests behind fences and ecstatic women in chastity belts." They broke into peals of laughter.

"To answer your question, think of people as coming from two basic cultural types: faithless dominators and faithful shapeshifters. The first don't believe that a higher power can be trusted to take care of the world. Their actions are guided by fear and distrust and a belief that they themselves must mold their destinies. They see human beings as positioned at the pinnacle of an evolutionary process that has ended with a man ruling over everything. Whatever is not male and human is mistrusted. Happiness is arrived at through materialistic consumption. They, the ones at the top, encourage and feed their sheeps' appetites. Anyone who does not adhere to their worldview must be 'convinced'—civilized—or destroyed. Faithful shapeshifters, on the other hand, believe in a higher power who causes all things to happen for reasons that humans may not comprehend but can accept as being for the greater good. Their actions are guided by trust. To their way of thinking, humans are part of the unity—no better or worse, no higher or lower, than the rocks, plants, animals, and stars. There is no evolutionary pyramid. They believe in the power of the dream—as a way to communicate with the Creator—and that to cause change we need only change our dreams. Since the Creator takes care of material needs, happiness is a matter of feeling our connectedness, our ecstasy. They live and let live, not trying to force their values on everyone else."

"Live and let live."

"Commercialism became a way of life for the faithless dominators, *the* way of life, replacing all other religions. It gave them more control."

"Amen!"

She smiled tenderly at me. "You understand. It was a good question. Now that it has been answered, you can return to your other world where you have work to do."

I started to rise up from their circle when she raised a hand, stopping me.

"One thing more. Hopefully you've learned this too. Never be afraid to ask, no matter how ludicrous the question—or the situation—may appear." She waved me up.

I rose slowly. The thirteen women watched me. They stood quietly, as though before a shrine. I noticed that some of the plants in their garden had sprouted leaves and flowers. The strong scent of night-blooming jasmine came to me.

Then all went black.

I felt a breeze against my cheek and something feathery brush my neck. I reached up to touch it. My fingers closed around a velvety branch. Pulling it to me I smelled the fragrance of jasmine.

The night was darker than before. Where the strobing star had been, there was only blackness. Off to my left was a flickering light which I knew to be that of Tsukanka's fire seeping through the spaces between the poles in the wall of his lodge. I started to stand but found my legs to be unsteady. Cautiously I rose to my knees, took a whiff of the jasmine, and stood up.

I made my way slowly into the lodge.

Tsukanka was standing beside the fire smiling at me. I had the distinct impression that he had been awaiting my return. Several men and women sat on stools around the fire. I went to him. He nodded, a big grin on his usually reserved face. He extended his arms and in the air drew a huge circle, a globe; he pointed through it at me. The people seated near him joined him in boisterous laughter.

Tsukanka stepped forward and touched my arms. We stared into each other's eyes for a brief moment. Then his moved to where I had laid out my sleeping bag. I bowed to him and made my way to it. As I crawled in, I was surprised to find that Ehud was already sleeping soundly on one side of me and Raul on the other.

Epilogue

Ureu-eu-wau-wau means "People-from-the-stars." In the language of a remote Amazon tribe, it is the name they have given themselves. According to ancient legends, whose origins have been swept away like the pottery shards of lost cultures, the Ureu-eu-wau-wau lived on a planet that orbited one of the six stars of the Pleiades. A princess among them possessed extraordinary powers of prophecy. She dreamed that the inhabitants of a distant planet, named Earth, were doomed; they would, she told her people, "consume themselves into extinction." Compelled by their compassionate natures, the Ureu-eu-wau-wau authorized a mission of mercy to take a message of salvation to the misguided inhabitants. The chosen emissaries—including the princess—were transformed into spheres of pure energy and sent on their way out into the darkness of space.

Approaching our planet, they were attracted to the place where plants, animals, and oxygen were most abundant: the Amazon forest. There they materialized into human form to await the time of the prophecy, when their message would be received and heeded.

A gentle people who practiced the arts of ecstasy, the Ureu-eu-wau-wau developed a culture based on faith and love. One of the most frequently used words in their language, *aba-a-bare*, symbolizes their values. The word has several meanings: "I love you," "The spirits of the forest bless you," "Glad to see you," and "May the good spirits forever guide you."

The industrial cultures discovered the Ureu-eu-wau-wau—and their forests—in the twentieth century. Miners, loggers, cattle ranchers, and machine-gun-toting soldiers swarmed into their lands. These men, the Ureu-eu-wau-wau knew, were the destructive ones foretold by the prophecy. They would not listen to the message, but perhaps they had come to set the stage for those who would.

Among these, there were a few who wore black robes and were different. They learned the language of Pleiades and had ears that could listen to a book. Many of the stories told by this book reminded the Ureu-eu-wau-wau of their own history, especially the one about a star that came to visit Earth and announced the arrival of a great messenger, a shaman named Jesus Christ.

Christ's message was rejected by the people of his time. He was humiliated and killed. Like him, the Ureu-eu-wau-wau understood the necessity of martyrdom. They suffered in silence at the hands of men obsessed with cutting trees and digging earth, "consuming themselves into extinction." Just as the followers of Christ had been tortured and slaughtered, so were the Ureu-eu-wau-wau. Their population was decimated. By 1997 only forty-three Ureu-eu-wau-wau survived.

"We came to deliver a message," one of those forty-three, a shaman named Ipupiara, told an audience of three hundred psychotherapists at a recent conference in Washington, D.C. "It is the beginning of a new millennium. Now is the time for you to listen!"

Ipupiara means "freshwater river dolphin," an animal who traveled from the constellation Dolphinus to Earth along filaments of light created from the tails of fiery comets. Able to slip into human form at will, dolphins serve as power animals, shamanic guides, and teachers of shapeshifting.

When Ipupiara was eighteen, a tribal elder ordered him to attend the white man's schools. "Learn about them so you can help change their dreams. Only in this way can we save our forests and all the species we love, including human beings. Only then can we accomplish the thing we came to do." Because at that time indigenous people had few rights under Brazilian law, Ipupiara adopted the Portuguese name Bernardo

Peixoto, became fluent in English, Spanish, and Portuguese (as well as eight indigenous dialects), and earned Ph.D.'s in anthropology and biology.

Ipupiara married a Quechua from the Peruvian Andes. His work took them to Washington, D.C. "Here," he said to his wife Jenny, "is where I must start delivering the message of my people." Eventually he was invited to serve as advisor to the Clintons at the White House, and to the Smithsonian Institute.

Back in 1993 I received a call from a woman who had read my first two books and also knew Bernardo Peixoto. "He is beside himself," she told me. "Please try to help." Over the phone I heard the sadness in his voice. He was distraught, he told me, because of the prohibitions imposed by the Smithsonian on the language he used. "In speeches I'm not supposed to talk about tree spirits, shamans, or the devastation caused by international corporations." In addition, he complained, the White House had gone back on its promise to listen to the message of the Ureu-eu-wau-wau. "In fact," he said, "they have lost interest in indigenous people and the environment."

I flew to Washington. I met a man in his mid-fifties who had the long, straight black hair and proud bearing of an Amazon native and wore the clothes and scholarly glasses of a Ph.D. anthropologist. The first time our eyes met we felt the strength of ancient ties. To honor that bond, we became blood brothers during a sacred Ureu-eu-wau-wau ceremony. In Ipupiara's words, "Now the Condor and Eagle can soar together and teach as one."

I helped him deliver his message, encouraging him to expand his circle out of Washington and into more receptive audiences. Sometimes we traveled across the country together, giving lectures and workshops and talking on radio and television shows. Our love grew over the years.

After my trip to the Shuar and Achuar, I turned to Ipupiara for advice. I described for him my visits with Tampur and Tsukanka and the journey back through time in the globes of energy.

"You have been honored by my ancestors," he said, after I finished. "You traveled in their shapeshifting canoes of light." We were strolling along the Mall, past the Smithsonian; he stopped to give me a piercing look. "What you saw is truth. Now you must act."

He pointed at the Washington Monument. "A statue to the People-from-the-stars, if ever I saw one!" We continued walking. "What an incredible shapeshift you experienced, brother!" His voice turned serious. "It happened with the Achuar for a reason."

Once again he stopped. "Honor them." He placed his hands on my shoulders. "You must embrace their request. Do as they instructed. Create a way to pay them and the Shuar to protect the trees from your own people. This responsibility falls on these shoulders." He tightened his grasp. "It is up to you to insure that the forests are there to absorb the carbon dioxide of the cars your people produce—the cars and industries—to provide oxygen for future generations." He let his hands drop and permitted the suggestion of a smile. "Air and water and earth and fire. Take heed. Find ways to materialize the dream of a sustainable future. Listen to Tampur's words about the Four Sacred Sisters. You know that it is true: Life cannot survive without the Four Sacred Sisters and they cannot survive without the forests. Follow the mandate of the elders' council. Act. I'll be at your side."

During the ensuing months, meetings were held in the Andes and Amazon and in Europe and North America. People from all the continents were invited. The intent was to establish some sort of organization that would provide a foundation for a new way of perceiving, a new paradigm, a shapeshift. In addition to indigenous people, attendees included participants from the workshops and trips; friends and followers of Marina Bellazzi, the Italian artist and student of Tibetan shamanism; doctors; entrepreneurs; lawyers; musicians; artisans; and others who were committed to changing the dream.

We decided that this organization should not be a formal one. Ideally, it should not be either a for-profit or a nonprofit corporation, since that would place it under restrictions imposed by the laws of some country. We agreed that it needed to be truly universal in character, a worldwide grassroots movement unencumbered by political, economic, and religious affiliations of any sort, motivated by a set of goals that could be simply stated, reflecting commonly shared values that would serve future generations—not just of human beings, but of all Pachamama's children, including the rocks, rivers, and mountains.

Once these general guidelines had been established, we got down to the job of defining the goals, settling on a name, and establishing an operating structure.

First came the goals. We reached consensus on three that would truly help the shapeshift: inspiring earth-honoring changes in consciousness, conserving forests, and applying indigenous wisdom in ways that foster environmental and social balance and a sustainable future.

Then came the naming. We went through several iterations and ended up with Dream Change Coalition (DCC).

Finally we brainstormed the structure. Dream Change Coalition would be like a philosophy or religion—anyone could belong, in the same way anyone can be a democrat, socialist, Christian, or Buddhist. Saying "I am a Dream Change Coalition member" would simply be expressing a belief in the three aforementioned goals.

A Shuar elder described Dream Change Coalition as "a seedpod that opens to Nace (the wind that blows through the forest), spreading its creativity across the land." A Quechua shaman piped in, "Faith and a dream is all that is needed to shapeshift everything." Their words reminded me of this question that is often asked at my workshops: "Are you suggesting that we here in New York City can return to the ways of our ancestors, to living like the Achuar?"

The obvious answer, of course, is that this is not realistic, but that we can return to more sustainable lifestyles, ones that emphasize ecstasy over materialism. Now for the first time I saw possibilities beyond that. I began to understand that we can in fact return to the principles upon which shamanic cultures are based. We can embrace the tenants of the faithful shapeshifters, the concept that things happen for reasons that we may not comprehend, yet can accept as being for the greater good; that there is no evolutionary pyramid; that we are indeed inseparable from the "other"; that the dream in all its aspects, both conscious and beyond consciousness, is our direct line of communications with a power higher than ourselves; and that happiness is not about production and consumption but simply a matter of feeling our connectedness, experiencing the euphoria of being. It seemed to me that such a revelation allows us to break through a barrier that has oppressed modern, industrial cultures for a long time, opening us up to the possibility of defining ourselves and our relationships outside the centuries-old limitations that have locked us into the shackles of fear, uncertainty, and the need to take control.

I also realized that just as dream change must occur on two levels— dreaming the change, as in the Tibetan star journey, and acting to materialize it in this reality—so too Dream Change Coalition had to be more than a cluster of people with shared values and goals. We had to organize ourselves in ways that would put the three goals to practical use. However, this realization appeared to contradict our commitment to a noncorporate structure.

One night, as I was falling asleep, the image of Knut Thorsen came to me. We were standing together at the window of his hotel room, looking out at the harbor of Ujung Pandang. Two Bugi prahus sailed past each other, their hulls dipping into the waves, as if in salute. "The corporation is a vehicle," he said. "A very powerful one. It can destroy us. Or be our salvation."

The next morning I made airplane reservations to the Yucatan.

The great stone pyramid rose out of the jungle, like a volcano, into the morning sky. It seemed part of the landscape, a cousin to the forest. Viejo Itza and I sat in the shadow between the wall of trees behind us and the massive pyramid in front. As I described the events of the years since we had last met, of my adventures in shapeshifting, his eyes remained fixed on the summit of that magnificent monument that he knew so well and that had endured the test of gods and men and time.

I completed my story and sat silently, awaiting his comments. The sun was rising up the far side of the pyramid, behind it and slightly to the left; its slow progress created fascinating patterns of light and shadow along the edges of the crumbling and irregular terraces. Every now and then a beam would catch a piece of polished stone and come flashing at us, blinding me for an instant.

"Well, you did it," he said at last.

I peered at him.

"You shapeshifted on a cellular level."

"Yes."

"It's what you wanted." He chuckled. "You were very certain about that when you were here before. I remember it well. We talked about the shapeshifter's role in the survival of the human species. You told me that the main threat to that survival was the business world—a composite of executives, politicians, advertising agencies, television, and the like. In short, corporations."

I agreed that I had said this, adding that I still believed it.

"When I suggested that you needed to shapeshift those things, you were disappointed. You told me in no uncertain terms that you were more interested in the physical, cellular shapeshift than the institutional type. You wanted to be the jaguar. But then you settled for a ball of energy." He paused.

"I did that."

"You did indeed. Do you still wish to be a jaguar?"

It was my turn to chuckle. "No. The ball of energy, the chair, the spear and bundle of herbs were quite enough. I think it is time to get back to the real work, the survival of our species—and all the others we are taking with us. You promised me I could do both. Physical and institutional. I'm ready for the institutional."

He laughed. "Good memory." He seemed lost in thought. "Did you learn anything from your experiences as a chair?"

I did not have to give this any consideration whatsoever. I had thought about it often and was clear about the answer. "It confirmed that we truly are all one, at the most basic and the most profound levels. If all people were taught to do this, human attitudes about hierarchies would quickly change. Shapeshifters can't be faithless dominators."

He smiled and nodded, then turned his attention once again to the pyramid. I watched it with him, observing the pools of light and shadow that ebbed and flowed across the stones, constantly intermixing one with the other. The longer I watched, the less I was able to make a distinction between the two. Where light had been, now there was shadow. Where shadow had been a second before, now there was light.

"When you're up there on the summit looking down," he observed, "it sometimes is difficult to tell where the forest ends and the clearing begins. Yet, when you're here, it's very easy." I thought about this, but before I had a chance to comment, he continued. "You mentioned a Dream Change Coalition program for saving forests. Can you tell me more?"

"Of course. We call it POLE. The letters come from Pollution Offset

Lease for Earth. It grew out of those talks with the Shuar Tampur and the Achuar elders, the idea that a standing tree is far more valuable than a cut one because the Four Sacred Sisters must have trees, and we all must have the Four Sacred Sisters in order to survive. At that meeting the Achuar told us to find ways to pay them *not* to cut the trees. POLE is what we came up with. I personally see it as just a start, one step in the right direction. It works like this." I explained that carbon dioxide is an extremely dangerous greenhouse gas that is threatening to change our climate and smother us in our own pollution. We produce it every time we drive a car, take a bus, or buy clothes and food that are made in factories. On average, every person in the world is responsible for the creation of four tons of carbon dioxide per year. This number is much higher in the more industrialized countries. I went on to describe how trees absorb carbon dioxide during the photosynthesis process, and how these two factors seemed tailor-made to offer us an opportunity to pay indigenous people to protect their forests. "We can calculate the amount of carbon dioxide absorbed by an acre of tropical forest. A powerplant owner or car manufacturer can purchase POLEs to offset the pollution their businesses cause. Or you, as an individual, can do this. The money pays people like the Shuar, Achuar, and Ureu-eu-wau-wau simply to caretake their trees, not to succumb to the temptation to sell them to lumber companies, oil drillers, or cattle ranchers. The cost is surprisingly low, and the benefit is beyond measure: It is clean air. Life itself!"

"Sounds like a major shapeshift to me!"

"You like it?"

"I certainly do." He thought for a moment. "Not just for what it is, but also for what it represents. There is no reason to assume that corporations must depend on producing and selling things that destroy. Selling standing trees—air—makes a lot of sense."

"Exactly." I mentioned that the concept could include protection of animal habitats, plants with potential medicinal benefits, seed banks, areas vulnerable to soil erosion, watersheds. "The list is only limited by imagination." Then I paused. "One problem though."

"What?"

"In order to do all this, we need a legal structure, something contrary to Dream Change Coalition's founding principles. It is one reason I am here—to seek your advice."

This brought a loud guffaw. "My advice! About legal structures! From an old Mayan peasant like me?"

"It's really a shapeshifting issue when you get right down to it."

"Aren't they all?"

"Exactly."

We sat in silence for perhaps fifteen minutes. I amused myself by studying the play of sunlight and shadow on the pyramid. The sun had revealed itself over a corner of a terrace near the summit. Then my attention was brought back closer to where we sat, distracted by a large lizard that had crawled out from somewhere and came to lounge on the bridge of light that had begun to materialize between the shadow of the pyramid and the dark wall of trees. It stared at us without moving, as if awaiting his words. Then suddenly it blinked, pumped its head up and down, swished its tail, and scampered off.

"Funny," he said, "How complicated we can make our lives."

I asked what he meant.

Ignoring my question, he asked his own. "When you take people on trips to Ecuador, what legal structure do you use? Who do they pay?"

I explained that I had my own company, Prydwen, named after the Celtic ship of knowledge. "A company dedicated to education, to changing the dream."

"A for-profit company?"

"Legally yes, because that simplifies matters. We're not asking for donations. We sell services—trips and workshops—and a few products, like incense and Shuar necklaces that are made sustainably. That gets complicated for nonprofits. But, actually, we never make a profit. All the 'profits' are reinvested through another company, a nonprofit called Dream Change Inc. The money goes toward promoting earth-honoring changes in consciousness and ways of living and protecting the environment."

"Sounds like a good system to me. Why not use Prydwen for selling POLEs?"

"Because Dream Change Coalition is not supposed to be part of a country or restricted by the laws of any."

He pondered this. "I don't see a problem," he mused. "Dream Change

Coalition doesn't have to be. Prydwen is the legal entity. The money is given to Dream Change Inc. to meet Dream Change Coalition's three goals." He paused, his face lighting up. "It's ideal—a model that could journey around the world, like the seedpod the Shuar elder described! Your friend Marina can form a company in Italy. Someone else in Indonesia. And Egypt. You all are legal in your individual countries, pay taxes, thereby contributing to social services, and yet all are joined by the common dream."

"That's brilliant," I said, catching his enthusiasm. "Lots of people selling POLEs, indigenous art, watershed and herbal medicine protection, and countless ideas we haven't yet imagined . . . making livings by shapeshifting themselves and their institutions. Some could be nonprofits, others for-profits. Dream Change Coalition would be like a big umbrella over the entire thing, sort of the guiding light."

"A globe of energy."

"A globe of energy." This stopped me. It took me back to that night deep in the Amazon rainforest. It was as though I were suddenly there again, dissolving into that blue globe, lifting off, watching the illuminated forest beneath me, the band of soldiers attacking the little clan huddled in their cave. But this time I could see the faces of Knut and Yamin, Toyup, Buli, the old Shuar man and woman who had saved my life back in my Peace Corps days, Maria Quischpe, Kitiar, and Tayu. They all came together before me, like swimmers in a dream, merging, separating, and merging again, until finally their individual faces dissolved into a globe of energy.

At that moment the sun lifted itself above the summit of the pyramid. For an instant, a halo appeared around the figure of the lone jaguar. Then a great burst of light flashed down, blinding me, forcing me to close my eyes. When I opened them, Viejo Itza was standing. Arms outstretched, his back to me, he was facing the pyramid. Through his open arms I could see the sun, the pyramid, and the jaguar, every cell in my body infused with their gifts of warmth, power, and energy.

Acknowledgments

The events described in this book actually happened. Names and certain other details about people, places, and chronology have sometimes been altered. This was done in order to protect anonymity where I felt that was important, or because individuals requested that I do so.

I owe a great deal to many people. Without them this book would never have been written. I especially want to thank the shamans and shapeshifters from around the world who have been my teachers and who have inspired me and so many others. It would be foolhardy to list them all here, but I do want to single out a few whose teachings were especially instrumental in elucidating the subject matter of this particular book (and whose real names are not given in the text): Maria Arcos, Juan Arcos, Charapa, Chumbi, Daniel Guachapa, Atun Juank, Jose Joaquin Pineda, Roberto Poz, Maria Juana Yamverla, Manuel Yamverla, Esteban Tamayo, Jorge Tamayo, and Jose Tamayo, Rafael Taish, Alberto Tatzo, Amalia Tuitsa, Bosco Tuitsa, Tukupi, Tuntuam, and Abu Xerxes. I also thank all those teachers who are named in the text. How can we, who owe our children's futures to you, honor you enough?

My wife and daughter have been my partners throughout, and have shared so much pain and ecstasy. Thank you Winifred and Jessica.

My grandmother, Nana, all those years ago got me started on this path—the journey within as well as the one to other lands. Her spirit has stood by me.

And you, Dad, whose courage this past year has been a guiding light. You who rose above your personal agony of watching Mom go through such a painful shapeshift out of this life, and in the process performed your own act of magical transformation. A teacher by profession all your life, you shifted into your own form of shaman this past year—at least for me. Thank you.

Kwan Sung and Chu Young Lee taught me the power of mind over matter; I thank you for the inspiration your lives have provided to so many generations.

I am grateful, too, to all my colleagues at Inner Traditions—more than I can possible name here. Your dedication to shapeshifting through words has served as a great inspiration to me. I especially thank Ehud Sperling, who was my companion and advisor throughout many of the adventures described in these pages and is publisher of four of my books. Were it not for Ehud, there would be no Dream Change Coalition. I also want to single out Susan Davidson. It is not often that a writer can have as his editor one whose life so exemplifies the subject matter of the book. Susan is a shaman in her own right, an agent of change who teaches people to transform themselves through dance as well as words.

Note on
Dream Change Coalition

Dream Change Coalition (DCC) is a grassroots movement that was inspired by the shamans—a living institutional shapeshift described in the pages of this book. Dream Change Coalition today includes people from many cultures throughout the world. Its three primary goals are to:

1. Inspire earth-honoring changes in consciousness
2. Conserve forests, and
3. Apply indigenous wisdom in ways that foster environmental and social balance and a sustainable future.

Dream Change Coalition serves as a model for corporations and other institutions. By example, it offers new ways of perceiving and working that are sustainable and it encourages people to make their livings through means that are earth-honoring. Its programs include workshops and seminars, educational materials, trips to some of the shamans spoken of in this book, POLE (Pollution Offset Lease for Earth), sustainably produced products, tribal celebrations, and many other activities that had not yet been imagined when this page was printed.

To learn more about Dream Change Coalition or to communicate with John Perkins, please contact:

Dream Change Coalition
P.O. Box 31357
Palm Beach Gardens, FL 33420
(561) 622-6064
www.dreamchange.org

Suggested Reading

Allende, Isabel. *Paula*. New York: HarperPerennial, 1995.

Ausubel, Kenny. *Seeds of Change: The Living Treasure*. San Francisco: HarperSanFrancisco, 1994.

Balick, Michael J., with Paul Alan Cox. *Plants, People, and Culture: The Science of Ethnobotany*. New York: Scientific American Library, 1996.

Blair, Lawrence, with Lorne Blair. *Ring of Fire: An Indonesian Odyssey*. Rochester, Vt.: Park Street Press, 1991.

Cahill, Thomas. *How the Irish Saved Civilization*. New York: Anchor Books, 1995.

Carey, Ken. *Return of the Bird Tribes*. San Francisco: HarperSanFrancisco, 1988.

Castaneda, Carlos. *The Art of Dreaming*. New York: HarperCollins, 1994.

———. *The Eagle's Gift*. New York: Simon and Schuster, 1981.

———. *The Teachings of Don Juan: A Yaqui Way of Knowledge*. Berkeley and Los Angeles: University of California Press, 1968.

Chopra, Deepak. *The Way of the Wizard*. New York: Harmony Books, 1996.

Coelho, Paulo. *The Pilgrimage: A Contemporary Quest for Ancient Wisdom*. San Francisco: HarperSanFrancisco, 1995.

Colby, Benjamin and L. M. Colby. *The Daykeeper: The Life and Discourse of an Ixil Diviner*. Cambridge: Harvard University Press, 1981.

Colby, C., with C. Dennett. *Thy Will Be Done; The Conquest of the Amazon: Nelson Rockefeller and Evangelism in the Age of Oil*. New York: HarperCollins, 1995.

Conway, D. J. *By Oak, Ash, and Thorn: Modern Celtic Shamanism*. St. Paul: Llewellyn, 1995.

Cowan, James. *Mysteries of the Dream-Time: The Spiritual Life of Australian Aborigines*. Bridgeport, England: Prism Press, 1989.

Descola, Philippe. *The Spears of Twilight: Life and Death in the Amazon Jungle*. New York: New Press, 1996.

Drury, Nevill. *The Shaman and the Magician: Journeys Between the Worlds*. London: Arkana, 1982.

Eliade, Mircea. *Shamanism: Archaic Techniques of Ecstasy*. London: Arkana, 1989.

Eisler, Riane. *The Chalice and the Blade: Our History, Our Future*. New York: HarperCollins, 1988.

Harner, Michael. *The Way of the Shaman*. San Francisco: HarperSanFrancisco, 1990.

Harrison, Regina. *Signs, Songs, and Memory in the Andes: Translating Quechua Language and Culture*. Austin: University of Texas Press, 1989.

Jamal, Michelle (ed.). *Shape Shifters: Shaman Women in Contemporary Society*. London: Arkana, 1987.

Kalweit, Holger. *Dreamtime and Inner Space: The World of the Shaman*. Boston: Shambhala, 1988.

Kane, Joe. *Savages*. New York: Alfred A. Knopf, 1995.

King, Serge Kahili. *Urban Shaman*. New York: Fireside, 1990.

Lamb, B. F. *Wizard of the Upper Amazon*. Berkeley: North Atlantic Books, 1974.

Lovelock, James. *Gaia: A New Look at Life on Earth*. Oxford: Oxford University Press, 1987.

Mander, Jerry. *In the Absence of the Sacred: The Failure of Technology and the Survival of the Indian Nations*. San Francisco: Sierra Club Books, 1992.

Markale, Jean. *Merlin: Priest of Nature*. Rochester, Vt.: Inner Traditions, 1995.

McIntyre, L. *The Incredible Incas and Their Timeless Land*. Washington, D.C.: National Geographic Society, 1975.

McKenna, Terrence. *The Archaic Revival: Speculations on Psychedelic Mushrooms, the Amazon, Virtual Reality, UFOs, Evolution, Shamanism, the Rebirth of the Goddess, and the End of History*. San Francisco: HarperSanFrancisco, 1992.

Mitchell, Edgar. *The Way of the Explorer: An Apollo Astronaut's Journey Through the Material and Mystical Worlds.* New York: Putnam Publishing Group, 1996.

Perkins, John. *Psychonavigation: Techniques for Travel Beyond Time.* Rochester, Vt.: Destiny Books, 1990.

————. *The Stress-Free Habit: Powerful Techniques for Health and Longevity from the Andes, Yucatan, and Far East.* Rochester, Vt.: Healing Arts Press, 1989.

————. *The World Is As You Dream It: Shamanic Teachings from the Amazon and Andes.* Rochester, Vt.: Destiny Books, 1994.

Popescu, P. *Amazing Beaming.* New York: Viking Press, 1991.

Quinn, Daniel. *Providence: The Story of a Fifty-Year Vision Quest.* New York: Bantam, 1996.

Rechtschaffen, Stephan. *Time Shifting.* New York: Bantam, Doubleday, Dell, 1996.

Rodriquez, G. *La Faz Occulta de la Medicina Andina.* Quito, Ecuador: Nucleo de America Ecuatorial, 1992.

Schultes, Richard E. and R. F. Raffauf. *Vine of the Soul: Medicine Men, Their Plants and Rituals in the Colombian Amazonia.* Oracle, Ariz.: Synergetic Press, 1992.

Stevens, J. and L. S. Stevens. *Secrets of Shamanism: Tapping the Spirit Power Within You.* New York: Avon, 1988.

Tatzo, A. and G. Rodriguez. *Vision Cosmica de los Andes.* Quito, Ecuador: Talleres Graficos Abya-Yala, 1996.

Tidwell, Mike. *Amazon Stranger: A Rainforest Chief Battles Big Oil.* New York: Lyons & Burford, 1996.

Van Hagen, V. *The Ancient Sun Kingdoms of the Americas.* London: Thames and Hudson, 1962.

Villoldo, Alberto. *Dance of the Four Winds: Secrets of the Inca Medicine Wheel.* Rochester, Vt.: Inner Traditions, 1996.

———— and S. Krippner. *Healing States: A Journey into the World of Spiritual Healing and Shamanism.* New York: Simon and Schuster, 1987.

Walsh, Roger. *The Spirit of Shamanism.* New York: Tarcher/Putnam, 1991.

Wesselman, H. *Spiritwalker: Messages from the Future.* Bantam, Doubleday, Dell, 1996.

Wolf, Fred Alan. *The Eagle's Quest: A Physicist's Search for Truth in the Heart of the Shamanic World.* New York: Summit Books, 1991.

BOOKS OF RELATED INTEREST

PSYCHONAVIGATION
Techniques for Travel Beyond Time
by John Perkins

THE WORLD IS AS YOU DREAM IT
Shamanic Teachings from the Amazon and Andes
by John Perkins

SPIRIT OF THE SHUAR
Wisdom from the Last Unconquered People of the Amazon
by John Perkins and Shakaim Mariano Shakai Ijisam Chumpi

THE STRESS-FREE HABIT
Powerful Techniques for Health and Longevity from the Andes, Yucatan,
and the Far East
by John Perkins

SHAMAN, M.D.
A Plastic Surgeon's Remarkable Journey into the World of Shapeshifting
by Eve Bruce, M.D.

DANCE OF THE FOUR WINDS
Secrets of the Inca Medicine Wheel
by Alberto Villoldo and Erik Jendresen

DON JUAN AND THE POWER OF MEDICINE DREAMING
A Nagual Woman's Journey of Healing
by Merilyn Tunneshende

THE SHAMAN'S DOORWAY
Opening Imagination to Power and Myth
by Stephen Larsen

Inner Traditions • Bear & Company
P.O. Box 388
Rochester, VT 05767
1-800-246-8648
www.InnerTraditions.com

Or contact your local bookseller